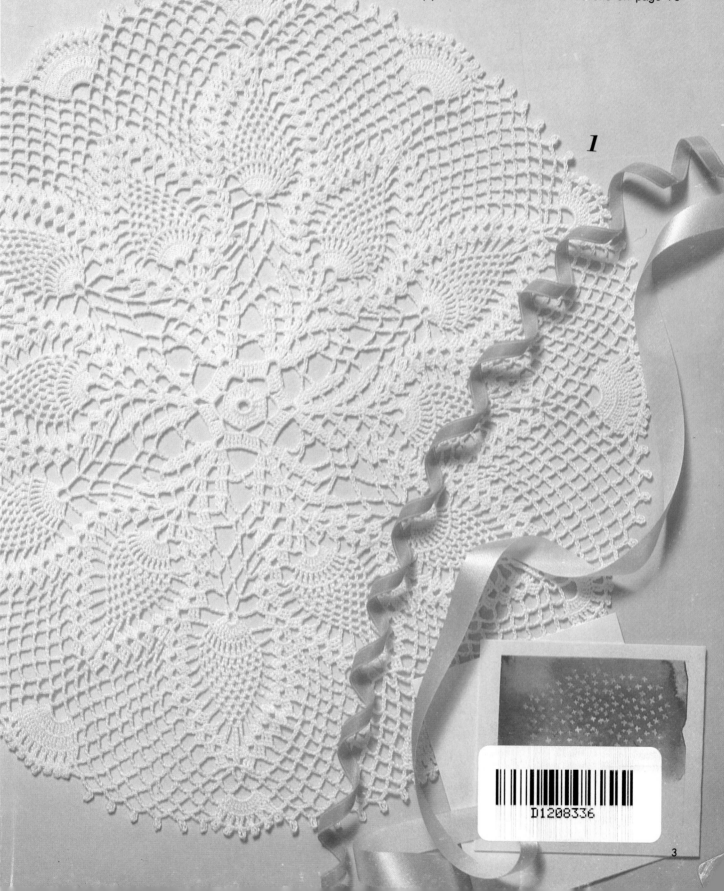

1

2

4

3

Refreshing, Entrancing Doilies

(2) Large 42 cm, medium 33 cm, small 22 cm in diameter   Instructions on 76
(3) 42 cm in diameter   Instructions on page 78

4

Graceful Pineapple=Pattern Doilies

(4) 32 cm in diameter Instructions on page 79
(5) 23 cm × 31 cm Instructions on page 82

5

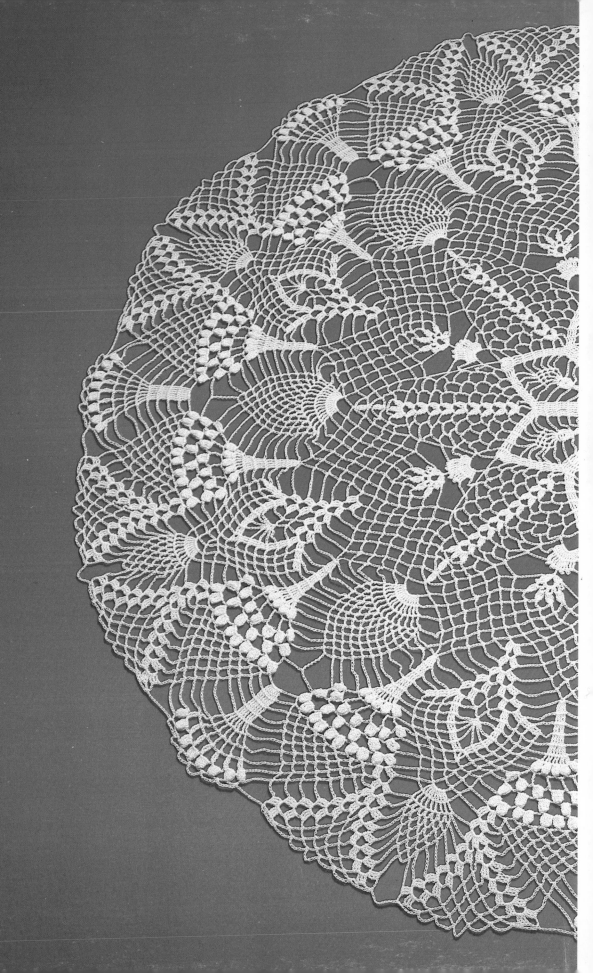

Large Elegant Doily

(6) 81 cm in diameter   Instructions on page 80

6

8

Doily Duet in Net and Pineapple Patterns

(7) 55 cm in diameter Instructions on page 12   (8) 52 cm in diameter Instructions on page 13

7. Shown on page 10

You'll need:
Crochet cotton gold DMC No. 40, 60g, white (298).

Steel crochet hook:
Crochet hook No. I

Finished size:
55 cm in diameter

Making instructions:
Ch-8, sl st in 1st ch to form a ring. **Row 1:** Ch-1, 16-sc in ring, sl st in 1st ch. **Row 2:** Ch-6, (1-tr, ch-2) 15 times in each sc around. **Rows 3 – 6:** Make 16 patterns with loops and tr. **Rows 7 – 14:** Work 32 patterns. **Row 15:** Work "2-tr at a time, twice and ch-14" 16 times in loop. **Row 16:** Work "19-sc, ch-2" 16 times in ch sts. **Row 17:** Work "1-dtr, ch-7, 1-dtr, ch-11 in the center of ch-19 and work 3-tr, ch-3, 3-tr, ch-11 in the center of the next ch-19" 8 times. **Rows 18 – 35:** Work pineapple patterns from Row 17. Work each pattern separately from Row 23. **Rows 36 – 49:** Join thread to Row 34 and work as shown in the chart. Work dtr and cluster of 5dtr in 3 square meshes between pineapple patterns on Row 38. Start the next pattern.

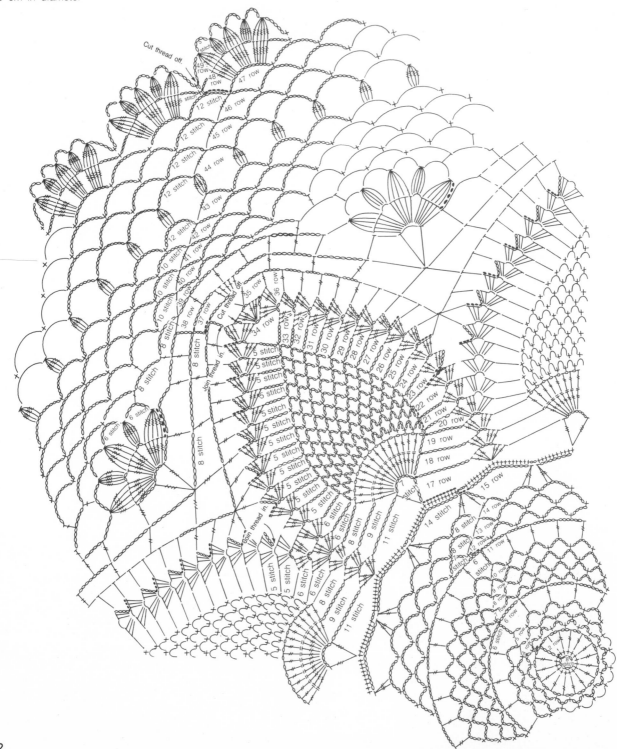

Work 12 patterns with puff on top of ch-3 on Row 7, 2-dc on top of 1-dc, ch sts between patterns. **Rows 16 – 25:** Work pineapple patterns in central ch-3 on Row 15 with yellow thread. Cover white thread with yellow one while crocheting. The yellow cotton end will be shifted to right to work next row. **Rows 26, 27:** White thread. **Rows 28 – 48:** Work leaf patterns (Rows 29 – 34) with green thread, and flower patterns (Rows 34 – 38) with yellow thread inside net st.

You'll need:

Crochet cotton gold DMC No. 40, 50g white (298), 10g yellow (236), 5g green (221)

Steel crochet hook:

Crochet hook No. I

Finished size:

52 cm in diameter

Making instructions:

Ch-10, sl st in 1st ch to form a ring. **Row 1:** Ch-3, 24-dc in ring, sl st in 3rd st of beginning ch. **Row 2:** Ch-6, "1-tr, ch-2" 24 times in each dc. **Rows 3 – 6:** Make 24 loops increasing ch st at every row. **Row 7:** Work 1 pattern in 2 loops. **Rows 8 – 15:**

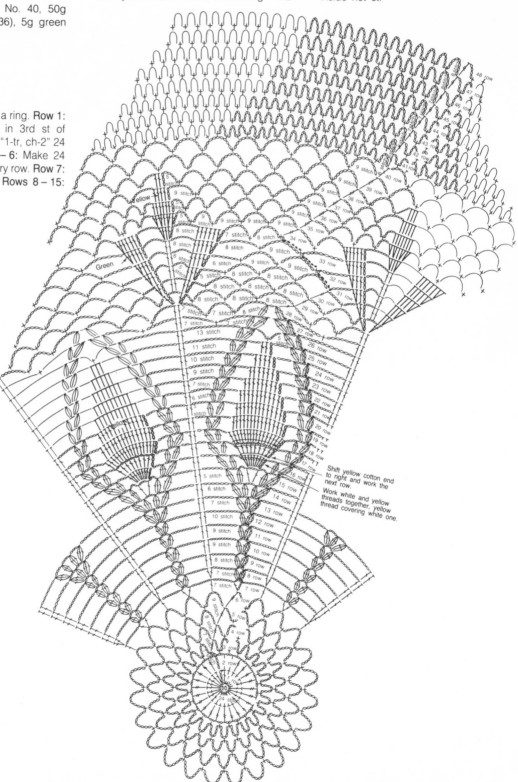

9

9. **Shown on page 15**

You'll need:
Crochet cotton gold DMC No. 40, 80g
white (298)

Steel crochet hook:
Crochet hook No. I

Finished size:
38 cm × 63 cm

Making instructions: *43*
Row 1: Ch-169, Ch-3, 2dc-puff, ch-3,
3dc-puff in the same ch st (3dc-puff, ch-3,
1 3dc-puff in the same ch st), 42 times in
every 5th st, and twice in both ends of ch
sts. Repeat the same on the opposite side.
Row 2: Work shell st of "3-dc, ch-3, 3-dc,
ch-7" in every 4th ch-3 on the previous row.
On both ends, work ch-1 in between shells.
Rows 3 – 13: In the same manner as the
previous row, increase shell sts at both
ends of Rows 4, 6 and 12 in accordance

with the chart. On Rows 6, 7, 12 and 13,
repeat shell sts around (100 patterns
around). **Row 14:** Repeat 11-dc and ch-7
and 1 shell st and ch-7 in the center of shell
st on the previous row. At 4 corners, work
shell st between 2 shells on the previous
row. Work 26 patterns around. **Rows 15 –
28:** In accordance with the chart, work
pineapple patterns in the position of 11-dc
on Row 14 with loops of 3dc-puff and ch-3.
Row 29: As shown work shell sts and ch-10
and ch-13 around.

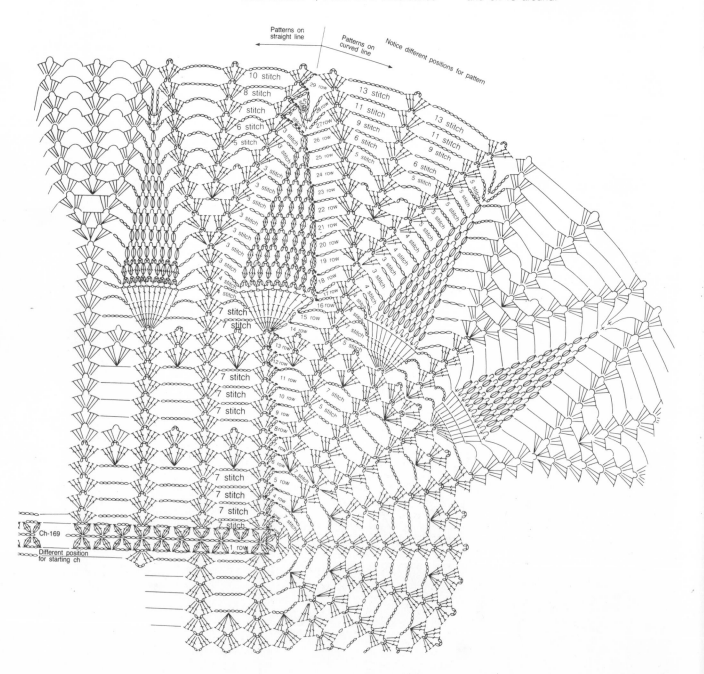

You'll need:
Crochet cotton gold DMC No. 40, 60g white (298)

Steel crochet hook:
Crochet hook No. I
Finished size:
41 cm × 60 cm
Making instructions:
Motif — **Row 1:** Ch-10, sl st in 1st ch to form a ring. Ch-11 (1-sc, ch-10) 7 times in ring, sl st in 1st ch st. **Row 2:** Ch-4, 1-dc, ch-5

(1-dc, ch-1, 1-dc, ch-5) 7 times in each loop. **Rows 3 – 5:** Work with ch, sc and dc as shown. From 2nd motif, work sl st at the center of ch-3 in 2 places to joint with the other motif. Work 5 pieces in the same manner.

Outside — **Row 1:** Work ch-10, cluster of 3-tr tr, ch-10 between motifs. Work 32 loops of ch-13 around. **Rows 2 – 7:** Work net st of ch-13, increasing 3 loops each on both ends of Row 2, and 8 loops each on both ends of Row 4. **Row 8:** Work 10-dc each in 16 loops on both ends, and 14-dc each in inside 11 loops. **Rows 9 – 27:** Work 1 pineapple pattern in 2 loops on Row 7. **Rows 28 – 32:** Start a new thread for each pattern.

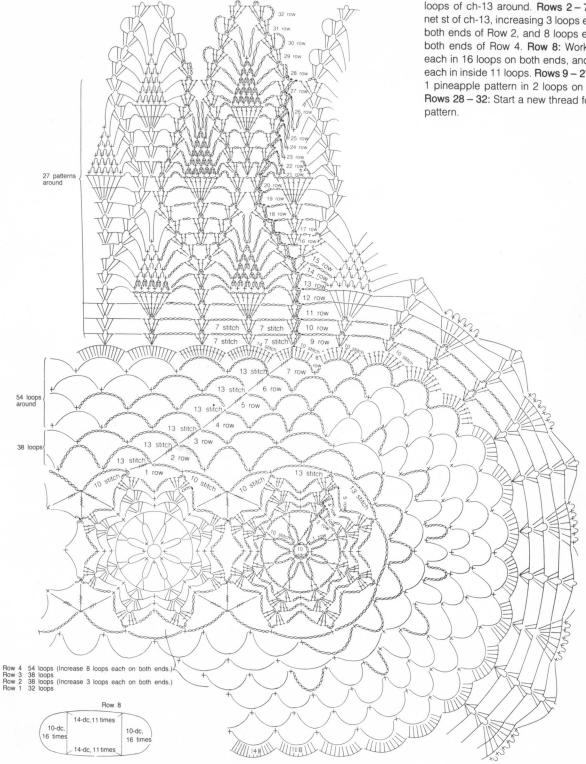

Row 4 54 loops (Increase 8 loops each on both ends.)
Row 3 38 loops
Row 2 38 loops (Increase 3 loops each on both ends.)
Row 1 32 loops

Row 8

| 10-dc, 16 times | 14-dc, 11 times | 10-dc, 16 times |
| | 14-dc, 11 times | |

Oval Centerpieces with Images of Tropical Flowers

---

(10) 41 cm × 60 cm   Instructions on page 17   (11) 43 cm × 65 cm   Instructions on page 21

11

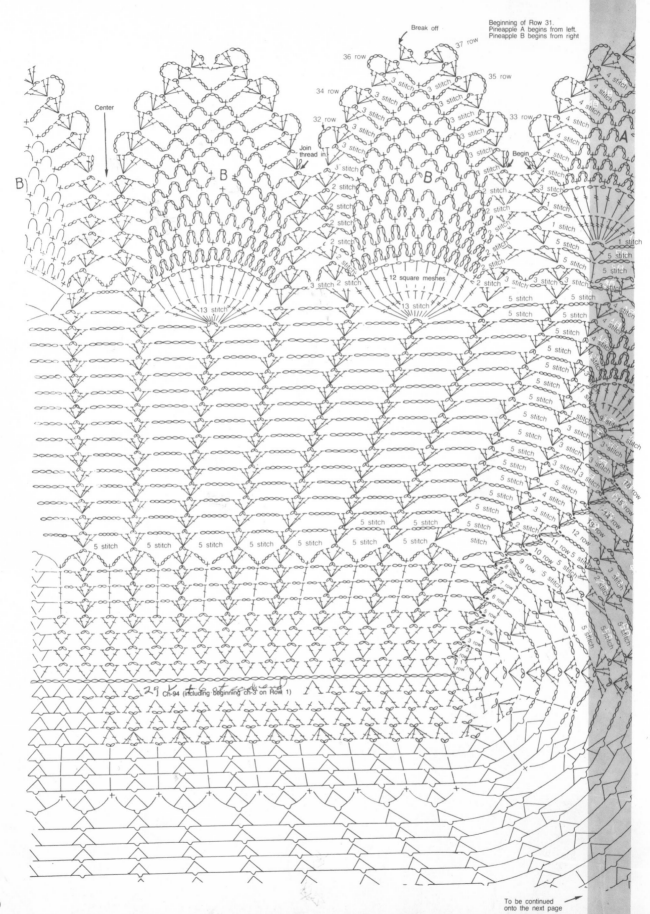

To be continued
onto the next page

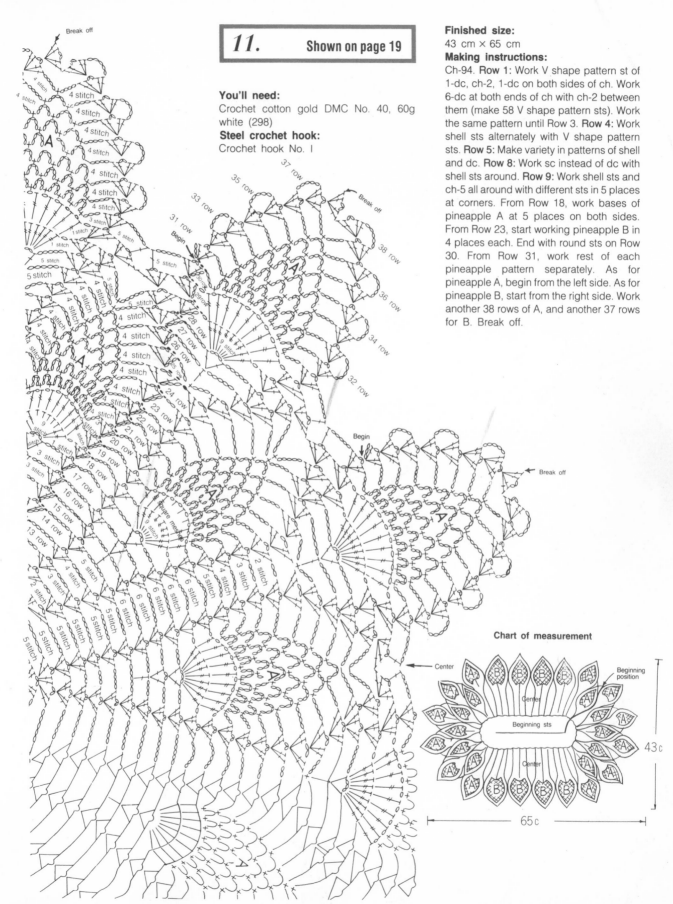

You'll need:

Crochet cotton gold DMC No. 40, 60g white (298)

Steel crochet hook:

Crochet hook No. I

Finished size:

43 cm × 65 cm

Making instructions:

Ch-94. **Row 1**: Work V shape pattern st of 1-dc, ch-2, 1-dc on both sides of ch. Work 6-dc at both ends of ch with ch-2 between them (make 58 V shape pattern sts). Work the same pattern until Row 3. **Row 4**: Work shell sts alternately with V shape pattern sts. **Row 5**: Make variety in patterns of shell and dc. **Row 8**: Work sc instead of dc with shell sts around. **Row 9**: Work shell sts and ch-5 all around with different sts in 5 places at corners. From Row 18, work bases of pineapple A at 5 places on both sides. From Row 23, start working pineapple B in 4 places each. End with round sts on Row 30. From Row 31, work rest of each pineapple pattern separately. As for pineapple A, begin from the left side. As for pineapple B, start from the right side. Work another 38 rows of A, and another 37 rows for B. Break off.

Chart of measurement

21

Centerpiece with the Glorious Scent of Flowers

(12) 72 cm in diameter   Instructions on page 24.

12

12. Shown on page 23

You'll need:
Crochet cotton gold DMC No. 40, 130g white (298)

Steel crochet hook:
Crochet hook No. I

Finished size:
72 cm in diameter.

Making instructions:
Row 1: Make a loop at the end of cotton. Ch-1, 8-sc in ring, sl st in 1st beginning ch st. **Row 2:** Ch-3, 1-dc, ch-1 (2-dc, ch-1) 7 times in each sc. **Row 3:** Work "ch-1, 1-sc, ch-10, 1-sc in 2-dc, and work 1-sc, ch-3, 1-sc in 1-sc" 8 times. **Row 4:** Work "5-dc, ch-7 in ch-10" 8 times. **Row 5:** Work "1-dc, ch-5, 1-dc, ch-3 in ch-7 and 1-sc, 3-ch-p (sl st at the end p, hereinafter referred to as picot), ch-3 in the center of dc" 8 times. **Row 6:** Work "3-dc puff ch-3 in ch-5, 4 times, then ch-3" 8 times. **Rows 7, 8:** Make 32 loops of ch-5 all around. **Row 9:** Work "ch-3, 1-dc, ch-5, 1-dc, ch-3 in a loop, 1-sc 1 picot in the next loop" 16 times. **Row 10:** Work "3-dc, ch-2, 3-dc (hereinafter referred to as shell once in ch-5 on the previous row, ch-5, and 9-tr and ch-5 in the next ch-5 on the previous row" 8 times. **Row 11:** Work "1-tr, ch-1" in shell and tr. **Rows 12, 13:** Make loops of shell and ch-5. **Rows 14 – 21:** Work 8 pineapple patterns separately. **Row 22:** Work "1-dc, ch-3" twice in shells on Rows 15, 17, 19 and 21 around. **Rows 23 – 34:** Work "3-dc puff, ch-2, 3-dc puff (hereinafter referred to as puff shell)," and work patterns in between puff and shell. **Row 35:** Work "3-dc puff, 1-sl st picot of ch-5, ch-7, and '(1-dc, ch-5) twice in ch-3' 9 times, ch-2" 8 times. **Rows 36 – 39:** Work shell of 3-dc, ch-2, 3-dc in every 5th loop on the previous row, and make 20 pineapple patterns around. **Rows 40 – 47:** Finish each pattern separately. **Row 48:** Same as Row 22. **Rows 49 – 59:** Work puff shells on top of pineapple patterns. Make 20 patterns. **Rows 62 – 65:** Work loops of shell and ch. Make 25 pineapple patterns. **Rows 66 – 73:** Complete patterns one by one. **Row 74:** Work "1-sc, ch-3" all around the outside.

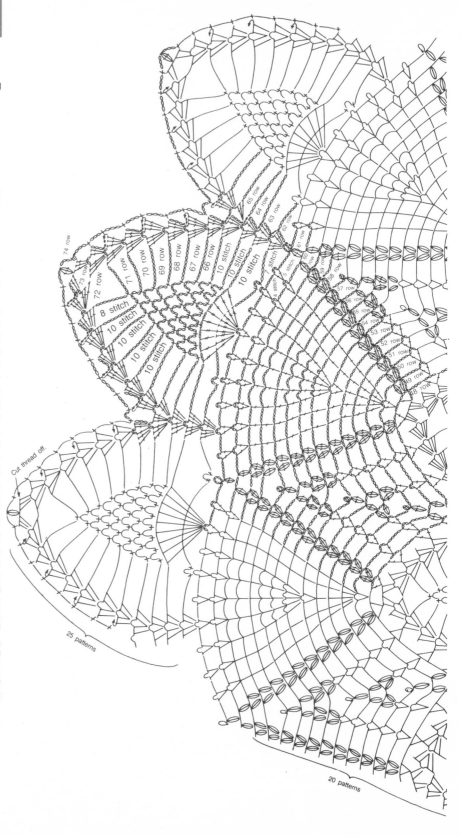

47 row
46 row
45 row
44 row
43 row
42 row
41 row
40 row
39 row
38 row
37 row
36 row
35 row
34 row
33 row
32 row
31 row
30 row
29 row
28 row
27 row
26 row
25 row
24 row
23 row
22 row
21 row
20 row
19 row
18 row
17 row
16 row
15 row
14 row
13 row
12 row
11 row
10 row
9 row
8 row
7 row
6 row
5 row
4 row
3 row
2 row
1 row

7 stitch
7 stitch
7 stitch
7 stitch
7 stitch
7 stitch
7 stitch
5 stitch
7 stitch
7 stitch
6 stitch
6 stitch
5 stitch

5 stitch
5 stitch
5 stitch

8 stitch

▲ = Join thread in.

Elegant Doilies Create a Rhythmical Pattern

(13) 60 cm in diameter   Instructions on page 28
(14) 48 cm in diameter   Instructions on page 32

13/14

13.

Shown on page 26

You'll need:
Crochet cotton gold DMC No. 40, 80g
white (298)
Steel crochet hook:
Crochet hook No. I
Finished size:
60 cm in diameter

Making instructions:
Ch-6, sl st in 1st ch to form a ring. Ch-1.
Work 16-sc in ring, sl st in 1st ch st. **Row 2:**
Work square mesh of 1-dc, ch-2 16 times.
Row 3: Work loops of ch-3 around ending
with ch-1 1-hdc. **Row 4:** Work square mesh
of 1-tr, ch-5 around ending with ch-2, dc.

Row 5: Make 16 loops. **Rows 6 – 10:** Make
16 triangle patterns of dc. **Rows 11 – 27:**
Work small pineapple. End off. **Row 28:**
Join thread at the place indicated. *Work 7
rows and cut thread off again on Row 34.
Row 35: Join thread to a loop of ch to work
pineapple patterns. Work until Row 52 and
sl st to end.

60 cm in diameter

Continued on the next page

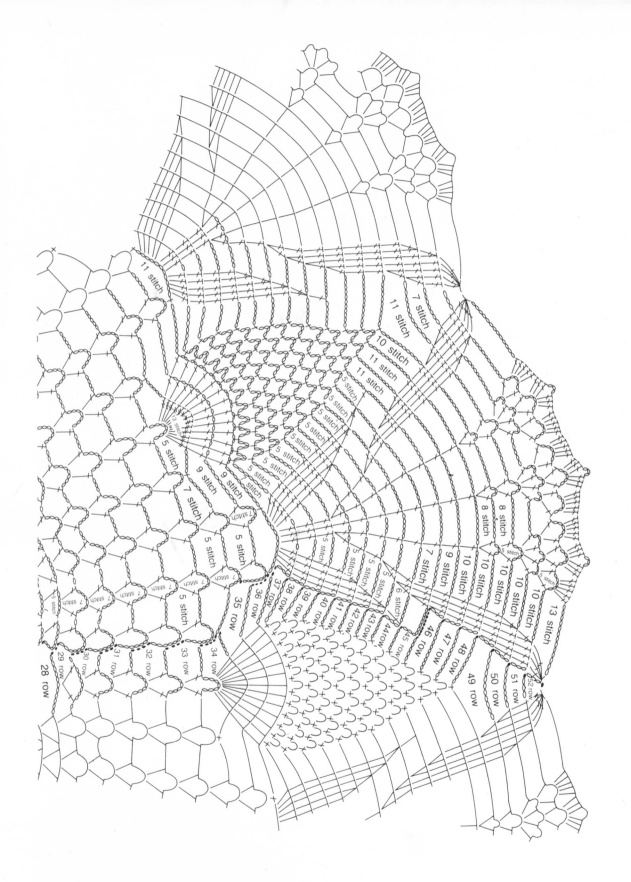

Classic Piano Cover and Pillow

(15) 61 cm × 193 cm Instructions on page 83
(16) 55 cm in diameter Instructions on page 33

15

14. Shown on page 27

You'll need:
Crochet cotton gold DMC No. 40, 40g ivory (206), 10g cream (204), some olive (238)
Steel crochet hook:
Crochet hook No. 12
Finished size:
48 cm in diameter
Making instructions:
Row 1: Make a loop at the end of ivory cotton. Ch-7, 1-qtr, ch-9, "2-qtr together, ch-9 (end with ch-4 and 1-dtr instead)" 14 times. **Row 2:** Work "1-sc (ch-4, sc picot of ch-3, ch-3, sc 3-ch-p) in loop of ch-9 and ch-7 (sc 3-ch-p, ch-3, sc 3-ch-p, ch-4) once" 15 times. **Rows 3 – 10:** Make 15 pineapple patterns referring to the chart. **Rows 11 – 14:** Use cream thread. Work V shape st of tr and ch. **Row 15:** Use olive thread and work in the same manner as the previous row. **Row 16:** Work 2-qtr together and ch around with olive thread. **Row 17:** Use ivory thread and work in the same manner as Row 2. **Rows 18 – 25:** With ivory thread, work 45 patterns following the same manner as Rows 3 – 10, however, on Rows 24 and 25 work sc 3-ch-p.

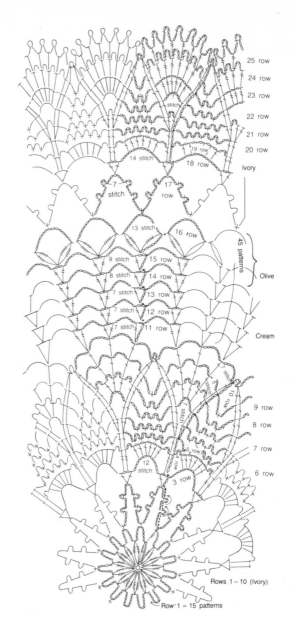

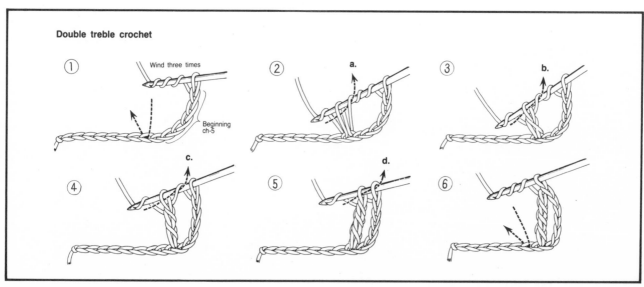

16. Shown on page 31

Crochet cotton gold DMC No. 40, 170g white (1), an inner-case of 53 cm in diameter

Steel crochet hook:
Crochet hook No. 4

Finished size:
55 cm in diameter

Making instructions:
Make a loop at the end of cotton. **Row 1:** Ch-3, 16-dc in ring, sl st in 3rd st of beginning ch. **Row 2:** Ch-8, (1-dtr, ch-3) 15 times in each sc. **Row 3:** Ch-10, (1-dtr, ch-5) in 2-dtr 15 times. **Row 4:** Ch-12, (1-dtr, ch-7) 15 times. **Row 5:** Ch-8, 1-dtr, ch-5, (1-dtr, ch-3, 1-dtr, ch-5) 15 times in dtr. **Row 6:** Work 15-dtr in "ch-3, ch-4, 1-sc in the next ch-3, ch-4" times. **Row 7:** Work "'1-dtr, ch-1' in 1-dtr 15 times ch-2" 8 times. **Row 8:** Work "'1-sc, ch-3 in 1-sc' 13 times" 8 times. **Rows 9 – 12:** Sl st 1-st at each row to shift the thread to the center of a loop. Decrease 1 loop each of pineapple patterns at every row, and work ch-5 between pineapple patterns on Row 11, ch-7 on Row 12. **Row 13:** Work "8 loops of ch-3, ch-4, 1-dc ch-4 in ch-7" 8 times. **Rows 14, 15:** Decreasing 1 loop at a time, work 3-dc in dc on Row 13, 5-dc on Row 15. **Rows 16 – 21:** Work "3-dc, ch-3, 3-dc" on top of 5-dc of Row 15 on Row 16. From Row 17, increase sts of ch in "3-dc, ch-3, 3-dc."

Start a new pattern from Row 19. Make "1-dc, ch-1 in 1-dc" 8 times, ch dc at the end. **Rows 22 – 31:** Work 9-sl st on Row 22, 8-sl st on Row 27 and proceed on to the next dc. Work 8 small pineapple patterns. **Row 32:** Work 3-sl st toward the center, work "'1-sc, ch-5, move to next loop' 6 times, 3-dc, ch-2, ch-5, '1-sc, ch-5, move to the next loop' 6 times" 8 times. End with ch-2, 1-dc. **Row 33:** Work net st. Repeat ch-7 once, ch-5 5 times, ch-9 twice, ch-5 5 times, ch-7 once all around (55 cm in diameter). Make 2 pieces of above.
Closing — (Row 34) Working "1-sc, ch-5 in loop" on Row 33 of each piece, insert an inner-case.

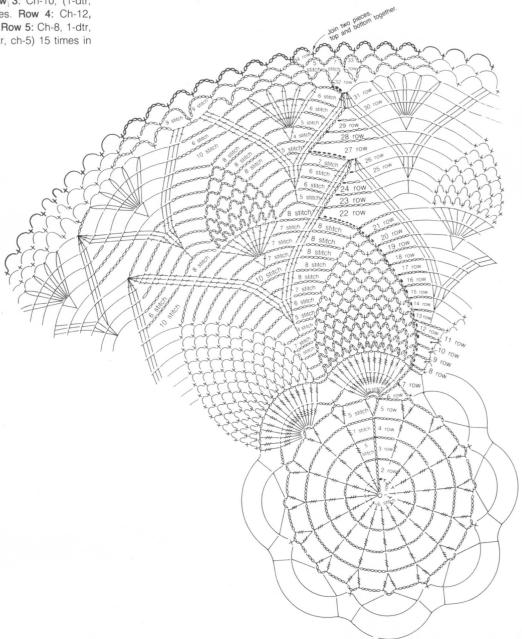

Neat and Attractive Tablecloth

(17) 65 cm × 145 cm Instructions on page 36
(18) 56 cm × 143 cm Instructions on page 86

17/18

17.   Shown on page 34

You'll need:
DMC Cotton A Pricoter, 330g white (1)
Steel crochet hook:
Crochet hook No. E
Finished size: 65 cm × 145 cm
Making instructions:
Ch-250. **Row 1:** Make 82 square mesh of

"1-dc, ch-2, 1-dc" and of filet crochet with 2-dc. As shown in the chart, work a pattern at both ends by increasing and decreasing sts. Until Row 124, work in accordance with the design chart. Then from Row 125, follow the design on Row 35 again till Row 136 (226 rows in total). From Row 227, work tip of flowers and leaves as shown. Work edging on one side. As for the counter side with 250-ch of the beginning, work edging in the opposite direction.

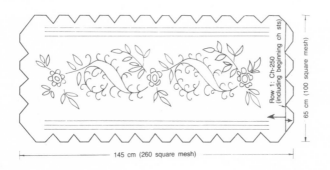

Row 1: Ch-250
(including beginning ch sts)

65 cm (100 square mesh)

145 cm (260 square mesh)

100

Beginning line

90

80

70

60

50

40

30

Repeat ← ②

20

10

80 70 60 50 40 30 20 10

Chair Backs and Centerpieces Creating a Pleasant Atmosphere

(19) 37 cm × 54 cm
   Instructions on page 87
(20) 45 cm × 65 cm
   Instructions on page 40
(21) 45 cm × 95 cm
   Instructions on page 41

19

20

21

20. Shown on page 38

You'll need:

Crochet cotton gold DMC No. 40, 100g white (298)

Steel crochet hook:

Crochet hook No. I

Finished size: 45 cm × 65 cm

Making instructions:

Ch-270 (including beginning ch st for Row 1). **Row 1:** Work 266-dc. **Row 2:** Work 5-dc each at the beginning and ending and work 86 square mesh between them. From Row 3, work patterns as shown. Sign × means filet crochet of 2-dc. Sign o which is a back of a butterfly will be quintuple-puff. Work two butterflies facing each other. Make square mesh on Row 127. Work dc on Row 128. Work an edging pattern of ch-3, 1-dc, 1-sc in each square mesh.

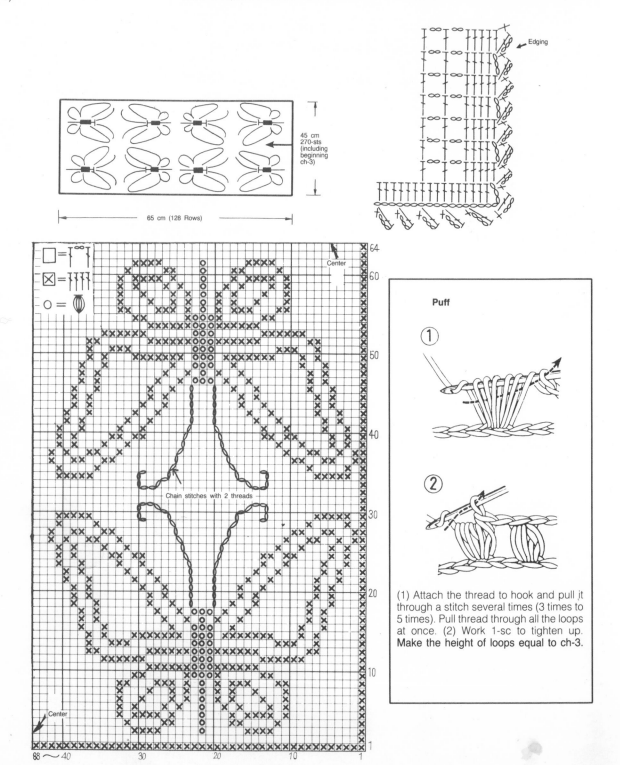

Edging

45 cm 270-sts (including beginning ch-3)

65 cm (128 Rows)

Center

Center

Chain stitches with 2 threads

88 ～ 40   30   20   10   1

Puff

① ②

(1) Attach the thread to hook and pull it through a stitch several times (3 times to 5 times). Pull thread through all the loops at once. (2) Work 1-sc to tighten up. **Make the height of loops equal to ch-3.**

21. **Shown on page 39**

You'll need:
Crochet cotton gold DMC No. 40, 120g white (298)
Steel crochet hook:
Crochet hook No. I

Finished size:
45 cm × 95 cm
Making instructions:
Start working from the center. Ch-249 including ch-2 for square mesh. Work patterns as shown. When one side is finished, work the other side starting from the beginning ch. As for edging, work 2-sc in square meshes of ch-2, 1-sc or top of dc, 3-sc at the foot of beginning and ending dc. Work 4-sc each in inclined sts.
Row 2: Work puff-cluster along the line of square meshes. Be careful in working uneven parts.

22

FASHIONABLE COLORFUL DOILIES

22.

Shown on page 42

You'll need:
Crochet cotton gold DMC No. 40, 15g reddish yellow (205), 10g white (298)

Steel crochet hook:
Crochet hook No. 12
Finished size: 25 cm in diameter
Making instructions:
Work with reddish yellow until Row 4. Cut thread off. **Row 5:** Change thread to white to work 2 rows. **Rows 7 – 15:** Work net st

with reddish yellow. **Rows 16, 17:** Work with white in the same manner as in Rows 5 and 6. Work 18 pieces of motif and join them together. **Rows 18 – 25:** Work net st. **Row 26:** Join motifs together, and work 2 rows around with white thread. **Rows 29 – 33:** Work with reddish yellow.

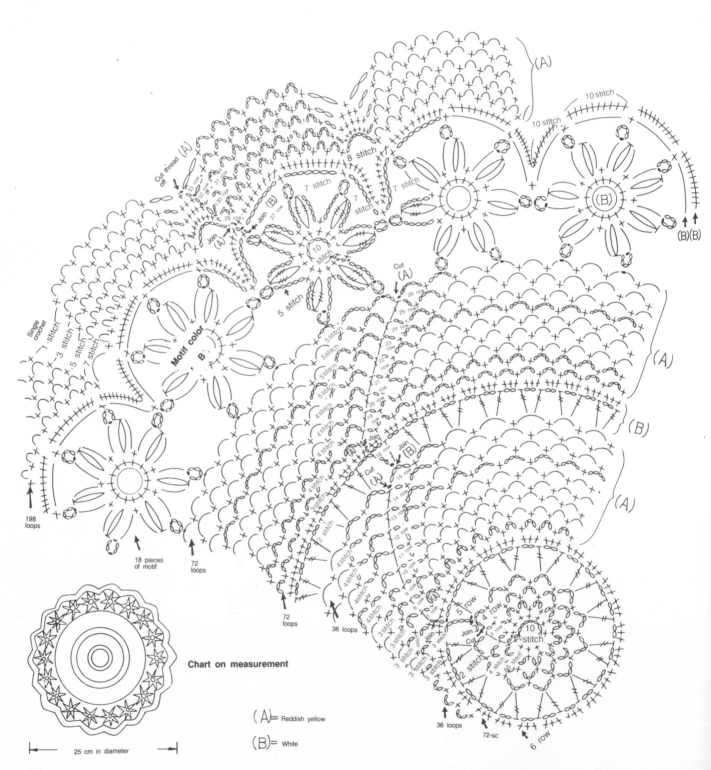

198 loops

18 pieces of motif

72 loops

72 loops

36 loops

36 loops

72-sc

Motif color B

Single crochet

1 stitch
3 stitch
5 stitch
7 stitch

5 stitch

7 stitch

8 stitch

10 stitch

10 stitch

Cut (A)

Join (B)

Cut (A)

(A)

(B)

(B)(B)

(A)

(A)

10 stitch

6 row

5 row

4 row

Chart on measurement

(A)= Reddish yellow

(B)= White

25 cm in diameter

44

23. Shown on page 43

You'll need:
Crochet cotton gold DMC No. 40. 10g dark pink (214), 10g pink (213), 5g light pink (201)

Steel crochet hook:
Crochet hook No. 12

Finished size:
38 cm in diameter

Making instructions:
Ch-8, sl st in 1-st ch to form a ring with dark pink. **Row 1:** Ch-6, 1-tr tr in one stitch, ch-9, (2-tr tr together in a stitch, ch-9) 7 times. **Row 2:** Work 4-sl st. Work "1-sc, ch-3, 1-sc, ch-8, move to the next loop" in loop of ch-9 on the previous row 8 times. **Rows 3 – 10:** Make arrow-wheel patterns increasing 1 loop of ch-3 at a time in the same manner as Row 2 (9 loops on Row 10). **Row 11:** Decrease one loop of arrow wheel at a time and increase another loop of ch-8. **Rows 12 – 15:** Decrease 1 loop in the same manner as previous row, and increase sts of ch in a loop of ch-8. **Row 16:** Repeat "work arrow-wheel in the same manner,

'ch-2, 1-dc' 7 times in ch-15 on the previous row, ch-2." **Rows 17 – 19:** Work in the same manner as previous row increasing sts of ch between dc. **Row 20:** Make ch-5 on top of arrow wheel, tr on top of dc, ch-7 around. Cut thread off. **Row 21:** Work 5-sc in ch-5 on the previous row, 8-sc in ch-7 with pink thread. **Row 22:** Make 23 loops of ch-3 on top of tr on Row 20. Join them with 2 loops of ch-7. **Rows 23 – 29:** Decrease 3 loops at a time from loops of

ch-3 in the same manner as the previous row, and increase 1 loop at a time in loop of ch-7. Cut thread off (end with ch-3, 1-tr instead of ch-7). **Row 30:** Change thread to light pink, and repeat "ch-3, 1-sc, ch-8, and 1-sc in next loop" in loops on the previous row. **Rows 31 – 34:** Work increasing sts of ch in the same manner as for Row 30. **Rows 35, 36:** Make loop of ch-13 and ch-14. **Row 37:** Work p at the center of a loop around.

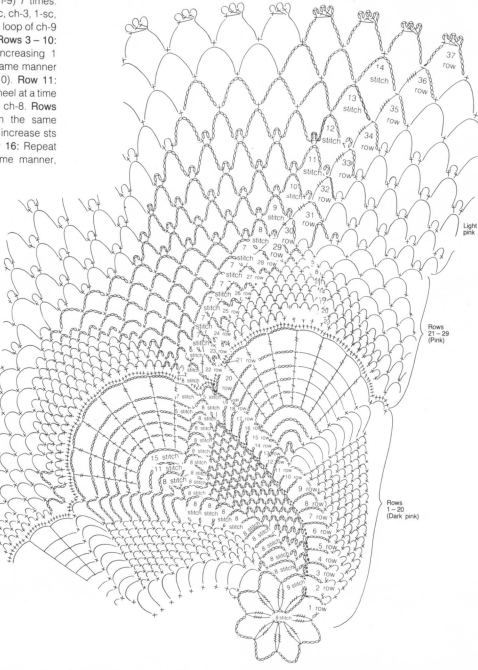

Light Refreshing Doilies

(24) 35 cm in diameter Instructions on page 48
(25) 32.5 cm in diameter Instructions on page 49

24. **Shown on page 46**

You'll need:
Crochet cotton gold DMC No. 40, 30g
white (298)
Steel crochet hook:
Crochet hook No. I

Finished size:
35 cm in diameter
Making instructions:
Ch-16, sl st in 1st ch to form a ring. Row 1: Ch-1, 24-sc in ring, sl st in 1st ch. Row 2: Ch-4, 1-tr, ch-4 (2-tr, ch-4) 8 times. Row 3: Repeat 6-tr, ch-3 in ch-4 on the previous row. Row 4: Repeat 8-tr, ch-4 on top of 6-tr

on the previous row. Row 5: Repeat cluster of 8-tr, ch-10, 1-sc, ch-10 on top of 8-tr on the previous row. Row 6: Work 16 loops of ch-12. Row 7: Work 5-tr, ch-6 16 times. Rows 8 – 12: Work sc, 2-dtr twice, ch. Rows 13 – 22: Work 96 loops. Rows 23 – 34: Work diaper patterns of tr and ch and loops with p.

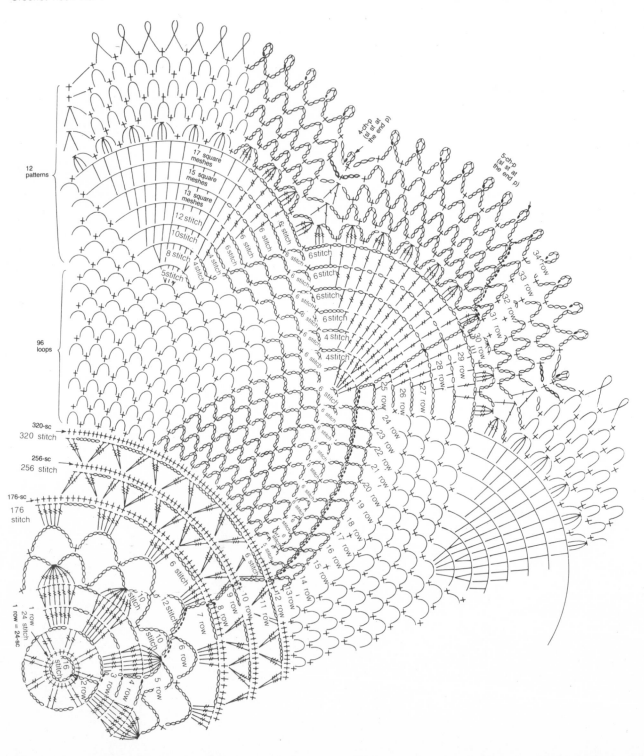

48

25. Shown on page 47

You'll need:
Crochet cotton gold DMC No. 40, 30g white (298)

Steel crochet hook:
Crochet hook No. I

Finished size: 32.5 cm in diameter

Making instructions:
Large motif (1 piece) — Ch-12, sl st in 1st ch to form a ring. Row 1: Ch-1, 16-sc in ring, sl st in 1-st ch. Row 2: Ch-7, (1-dc, ch-4) in every other sc on the previous row 7 times. Row 3: Ch-4, 5-tr (6-tr) in ch-4 on the previous row, ch-3. Row 4: Work 1-tr each in 6-tr on the previous row, ch-6. Row 5: Work cluster of tr-6 in 6-tr on the previous row, ch-12, and work 1-sc in ch-6, ch-12.

Small motif (8 pieces) — Work in the same manner as large motif. Omit Row 4 of large motif. Work ch-8 instead of ch-12 on Row 5. Join with a large motif after working clusters.

Outside — Work net st and cluster of 3-dtr to make leaf patterns outside of small motifs. Work sc around on the last row.

1 row = 16-sc

49

Simple, Neat Chevron=Pattern Doilies

26/27

(26) 40 cm in diameter Instructions on page 52
(27) 38 cm in diameter Instructions on page 53

26. Shown on page 50

You'll need:
Crochet cotton gold DMC No. 40, 40g white (298)

Steel crochet hook:
Crochet hook No. I

Finished size:
40 cm in diameter

Making instructions:
Ch-14, sl st in 1st ch to form a ring. **Row 1:** Ch-1, 28-sc in ring, sl st in 1st ch. **Row 2:** Ch-6 (1-tr, ch-2) 13 times in every other sc on the previous row, sl st in 4th st of beginning ch. **Row 3:** Ch-4, 13-tr, sl st in 4th st of beginning ch. Repeat "ch-3, 2-tr in next ch-2." **Rows 4 – 6:** Ch-4, repeat ch-4, 1-tr in ch on the previous row and 1-tr in next tr. **Row 7:** Ch-4, repeat ch-5, 1-tr in ch on the previous row and 1-tr in next tr. **Row 8:** Ch-4, repeat ch-6, 1-tr in ch on the previous row and 1-tr in next tr. **Row 9:** Ch-4, repeat "ch-4, 1-tr in ch-6 on the previous row, ch-4, 1-tr in from the 3rd tr to 7th tr on the previous row." **Row 10:** Ch-4, repeat "ch-4, '2tr in ch-4 on the previous row,' 1-tr in the next tr, '2-tr in ch-4 on the previous row' once, ch-4, 1-tr in each 3rd to 5th tr of 5-tr on the previous row." **Rows 11 – 17:** Work diaper pattern of tr on 5-tr on Row 10. Work square meshes of ch-4 and tr between patterns. **Row 18:** Work (1-tr ch-4) 98 times. **Row 19:** Work 4-sc in each ch-4 on the previous row. **Row 20:** Repeat 1-tr, ch-2 in every other sc on the previous row. **Row 21:** Repeat 1-sc ch-7 in every other square mesh on the previous row 98 times. **Row 22:** Work 1-sc, ch-7, and 1-sc in the next loop, "2-tr, ch-3, 2-tr" in the next loop. Repeat 14 times. **Rows 23 – 32:** Work 3-tr on "2-tr, ch-3, 2-tr" to make 14 chevron patterns. Decrease 1 inside loop of chevron pattern at every row, and increase outside 1 square mesh at every row. **Row 33:** Work cluster 6-tr on top of chevron pattern, ch-4, 1-tr, "ch-3, 3-ch sc-p, ch-3, 2-tr together in a stitch" 9 times, ch-3, 3-ch sc-p, ch-3, 1-tr, ch-4.

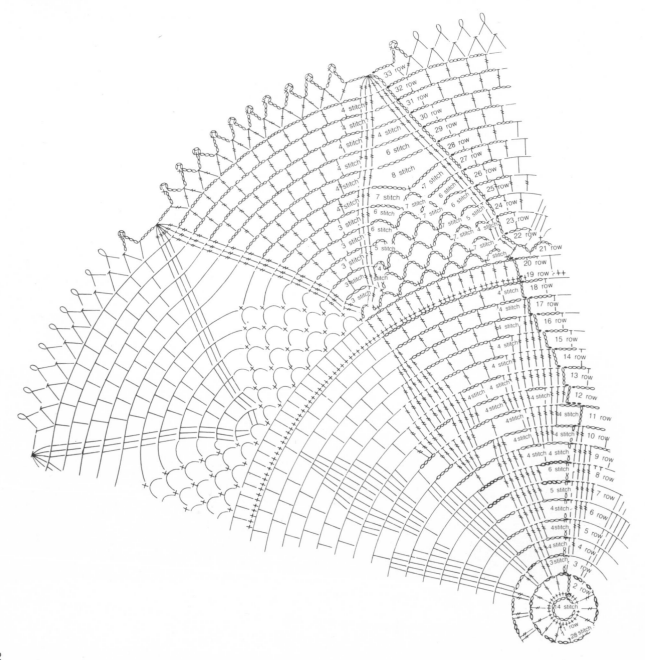

27. **Shown on page 51**

You'll need:
Crochet cotton gold DMC No. 40, 30g
white (298)
Steel crochet hook:
Crochet hook No. I
Finished size:
38 cm in diameter
Making instructions:
C-12, sl st in 1st ch to form a ring. **Row 1:**

Ch-3, 23-dc in ring, sl st in 3rd st of beginning ch. **Row 2:** Ch-4 (1-dc, ch-1) 23 times. **Row 3, 4:** Ch-1, "1-sc in ch, ch-5" 23 times, 1-sc, ch-2, 1-dc. **Row 5:** Ch-3, 1-dc at a time, ch-3 (2-dc together, ch-3) 23 times. **Row 6:** Ch-3, 2-dc together, ch-4 (3-dc together in ch, ch-4) 23 times. **Row 7:** Repeat 3-dc together, ch-5. **Row 8:** Repeat 3-dc together, ch-6. **Row 9:** Repeat 3-dc together, ch-7. **Row 10:** Ch-3, 8-dc, ch-1 (9-dc in ch on the previous row, ch-1) 23 times. **Row 11:** Ch-3, 7-dc, ch-3, 8-dc, ch-2

(8-dc, ch-3, 8-dc, ch-2) 11 times. **Rows 12 – 19:** At both ends of (8-dc, ch-3, 8-dc, ch-2) decrease 1-dc at every row and work new dc patterns between dc. **Row 20:** Work 7-sl sts. Make "'1-dc, ch-2, 1-dc' once, ch-3 (1-dc, 2-ch) 7 times, 1-dc, ch-3 (1-dc, ch-2) once, ch-5" 12 times. **Row 21:** Work 3-tr in each central ch on the previous row. **Row 22:** Work "'1-dc, ch-3' twice (3-tr together, ch-5) 6 times, 3-tr together, ch-3" 12 times. **Rows 23 – 27:** Work net st increasing sts of ch.

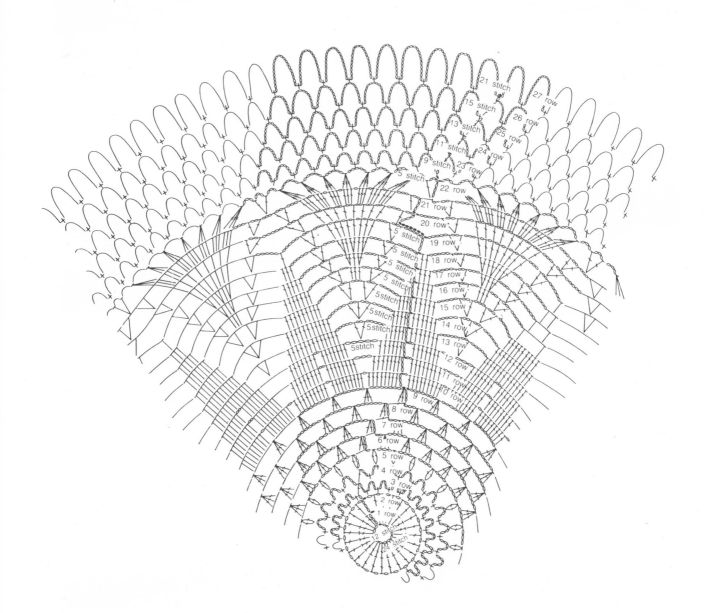

Centerpieces of Dainty Flowers

(28) 44 cm × 66 cm   Instructions on page 56
(29) 44 cm × 70 cm   Instructions on page 60

You'll need:
Crochet cotton gold DMC No. 40, 90g white (298)
Steel crochet hook:
Crochet hook No. I
Finished size:
46 cm × 66 cm
Making instructions:
Motif — Ch-10, sl st in 1st ch to form a ring.
Row 1: Ch-1, 16-sc in ring, sl st in 1st ch.
Row 2: Ch-7 (1-dc in every other sc on the previous row, ch-4) 7 times, sl st in 3rd st of beginning ch. Row 3: Ch-3, 3-dc, ch-10 (4-dc in ch-4 on the previous row) 7 times, sl st in 3rd st of beginning ch. Row 4: Work sl st of 2nd st of 4-dc on the previous row, ch-1, "1-sc in the center of 4-dc, 7-dc in ch-10, ch-5, 7-dc" 8 times, sl st in 1st ch. Row 5: Sl st to the center of ch-5 on the previous row, ch-1, "1-sc in the center of ch-5, ch-15" 8 times, sl st in 1st ch. Row 6: Ch-1, work "1-sc in sc on the previous row, ch-7, '1-sc, ch-7' 3 times in ch-15 on the previous row" 8 times. Rows 7, 8: Sl st towards the center of loops on the previous row, ch-1, sl-1 in the same loop, ch-7, "1-sc in the next loop, ch-7" 31 times, sl st in 1st ch. Row 9: Work sl st in the center of a loop on the previous row, ch-1, 1-sc in the same loop, then work "ch-11, 1-sc in the next loop, ch-5, 1-sc in the next loop," sl st in 1st ch. Row 10: Work 1-sl st, and repeat "7-dc in loop of ch-11, ch-5, 7-dc, 1-sc in loop of ch-5," sl st in 1st ch.

Joining — From 2nd motif, join to other motifs at the center of ch-5 on Row 10 by working sl st.

Piece — Same as Rows 1 – 4. Join them in the middle of ch-5 on Row 4.

56

30. Shown on page 58

You'll need:
Crochet cotton gold DMC No. 40, 10g
white (298), 259g yellow gradation (253)
Steel crochet hook:
Crochet hook No. I
Finished size:
21 cm × 32 cm

Making instructions:
Make a loop at the end of cotton. Work
ch-3, dc and 3-ch-p in ring, sl st in 3rd st of
beginning ch. Cut thread off. From Row 2,
use white thread until Row 5. Cut thread
off. From 2nd motif, join heads of p by
working sl st. Assemble 20 pieces as
shown in the chart on measurement, joining pieces in 11 places. Make a loop at the
end of white cotton. **Row 1:** Ch-1, 16-sc in
ring, sl st in 1st ch. **Row 2:** Work "1-sc,
ch-7, sc in between motif, 5-sl sts in ch
worked on the row ch-2."

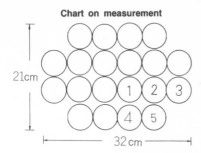

Chart on measurement

21cm

32cm

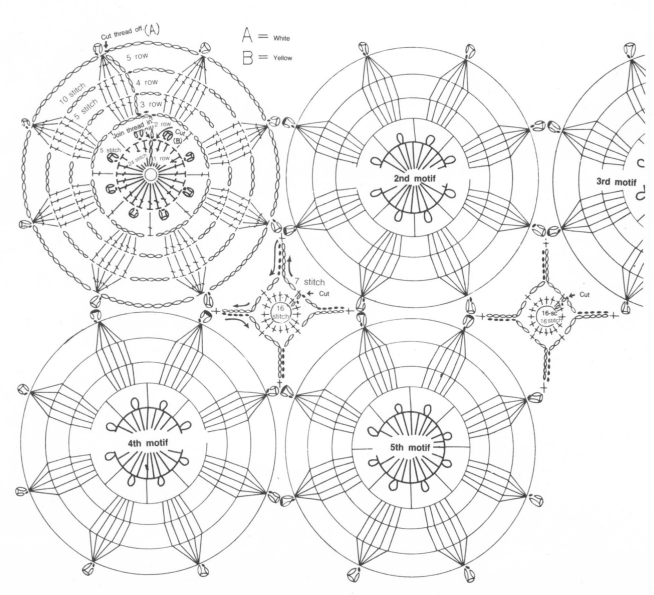

A = White
B = Yellow

Flowered Tray Cloth and Centerpiece

(30) 21 cm × 32 cm   Instructions on page 57
(31) 35 cm × 45 cm   Instructions on page 60

29. Shown on page 55

You'll need:
Crochet cotton gold DMC No. 40, 80g
white (298)
Steel crochet hook:
Crochet hook No. J

Finished size:
44 cm × 77 cm
Making instructions:
Motif — Ch-6, sl st in 1st ch to form a ring.
Row 1: Ch-1, 12-sc in ring, sl st in 1st ch.
Row 2: Ch-6 (1-dc, ch-3) 11 times. **Row 3:**
Ch-1, "2-sc, 3-ch-p, 2-sc" in loop of ch-3
on the previous row. Cut thread off. (4 cm
in diameter)
Joining motif — From 2nd motif, join at 2
places working "ch-1, 1-sl st in front p,
ch-1" instead of making p on Row 3. In the
same manner, join 11 motifs in line. Make

14 lines.
Joining lines of motif — Referring to the
chart, join thread to p, ch-8, repeat "sc-1 in
the next p, ch-5, 1-sc in the next p, ch-5,
2-dc together in 2-p (2nd p is the p in next
motif), ch-5." End with 1-dc. Cut thread off.
As for 2nd line of motifs, following the same
procedure, joint thread to p, ch-5, 1-sl st in
loop of 1st line, ch-2, repeat "1-sc in the
next p, ch-2, 1-sl st in the next loop, ch-2,
1-sc in next p, ch-2, 1-sl st in loop, ch-2,
2-dc together in next 2-p, ch-2." End with
1-dc. Join 14 lines in the same manner.

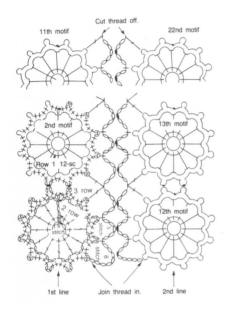

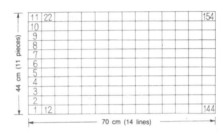

31. Shown on page 59

You'll need:
Crochet cotton gold DMC No. 40, 90g
white (298)
Steel crochet hook:
Crochet hook No. I
Finished size:
35 cm × 45 cm (Motif 5 cm × 5 cm)
Making instructions:
Ch-8, sl st in 1st ch to form a ring. Row 1:
Ch-1, 16-sc in ring, sl st in 1st ch. Row 2:
Repeat "1-dc (beginning with ch-3) ch-3,
1-dc in the same st, ch-3, 1-sc in the 3rd sc
on the previous row, ch-3, move to the 5th

sc on the previous row" 4 times. **Row 3:**
Work sl st through ch-3, repeat "4-dc
(beginning with ch-3), ch-3, 4-dc, ch-3,
1-sc in sc on the previous row, ch-3." **Row
4:** Work sl st through 3-dc and ch-1, "1-dc
(beginning with ch-3) in ch-3, ch-3, 1-tr,
ch-5, 1-tr, ch-3, 1-dc, 1-tr in next sc, ch-3,
1-dtr, ch-4, 1-dtr, ch-3, 1-tr" 4 times. **Row
5:** Ch-1, work "'1-sc 1-hdc, 3-dc' in ch-3,
1-dc in the next, 2-tr, '2-dc, 2-tr, ch-3, 2-tr,
2-dc' in loops of ch-5, 1-dc in the next tr,
'3-dc, 1-hdc, 1-sc' in ch-3, '1-sc, 1-hdc,
1-dc' in the next ch-3, 1-dc in the next dtr,
'3-dc, ch-3, 3-dc' in ch-4, 1-dc in the next
dtr, '1-dc, 1-hdc, 1-sc' in the next ch-3" 4
times.
Joining — From the 2nd motif, work ch-1,
1-sc ch-1 instead of ch-3 for joining.

32.   **Shown on page 62**

You'll need:
Crochet cotton gold DMC No. 40, 480g
ivory (206)
Steel crochet hook:
Crochet hook No. J
Finished size:
141 cm × 155 cm
Making instructions:
Ch-8, sl st in 1st ch to form a ring. **Row 1:**
Ch-3, 2-tr, ch-2 (3-tr, ch-2) 5 times to make
the base for a hexagon. From Row 2, make
6 patterns. From Row 10, work clusters of
6-tr in corners. **Row 14:** End with tr sts.
Row 15: Work dc instead of tr, except 1-tr
in 6 corners. **Row 20:** Work cluster of 4-dc
in all square meshes around. **Row 21:**
Repeat "1-sc, ch-4, 2-tr, ch-7, 2-tr, ch-4"
for edging. Break off. Work remaining 18
pieces in the same manner. From the 2nd
motif, join centers of ch-7 on Row 21 with
sc.

Chart on measurment

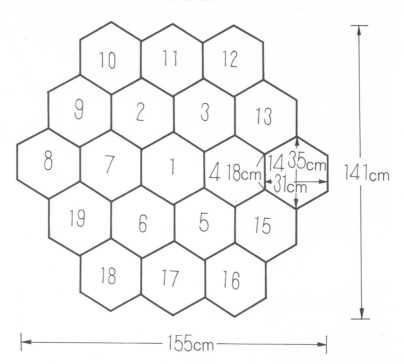

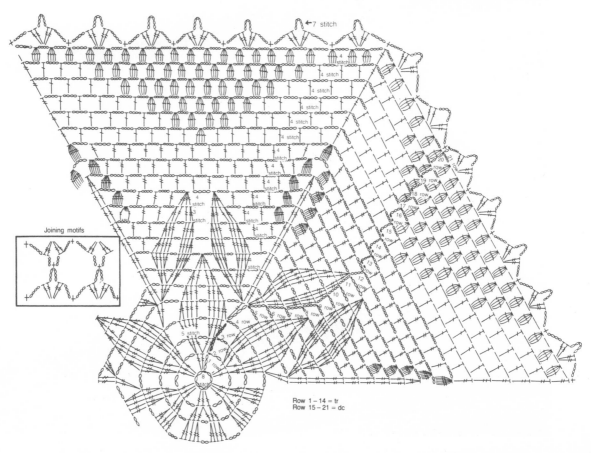

Joining motifs

Row 1 – 14 = tr
Row 15 – 21 = dc

33. Shown on page 66

You'll need:
Crochet cotton No. 50, 25g white
Steel crochet hook:
Crochet hook No. I
Making instructions:
Ch-135, sl st in 1st ch to form a ring. Work

45 square meshes of "ch-2, 1-dc." Work pineapple patterns until Row 20. Start making thumb from Row 21. From Row 30, work a little finger. Join thread to ch of the little finger to work 3 fingers together. Then, work the third finger. Join thread to ch of middle finger to work an index finger. Lastly, work 9-dc, 2-sc on 1st row and make loop of ch-4 on 2nd row around wrist.

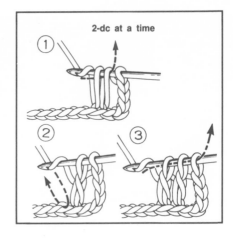

2-dc at a time

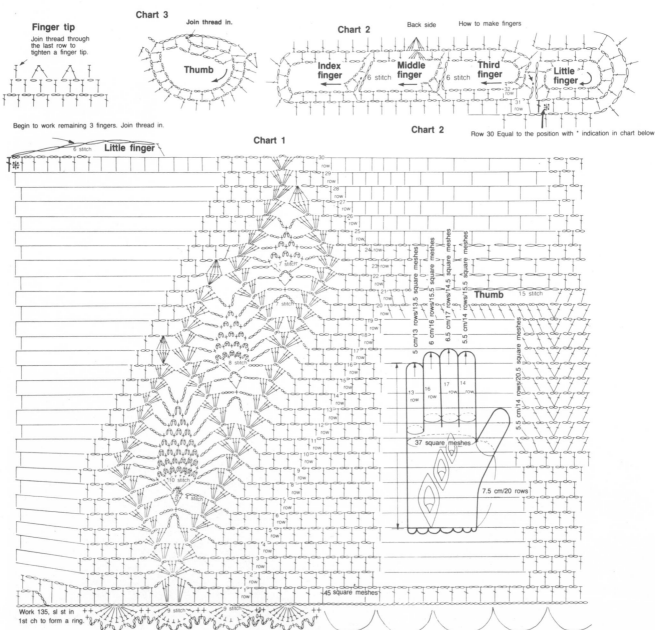

Finger tip
Join thread through the last row to tighten a finger tip.

Begin to work remaining 3 fingers. Join thread in.

Chart 3

Join thread in.

Thumb

Chart 2

Back side   How to make fingers

Index finger   Middle finger   6 stitch   Third finger   Little finger

6 stitch

Chart 2

Row 30 Equal to the position with * indication in chart below

Little finger   6 stitch

Chart 1

45 square meshes

Work 135, sl st in 1st ch to form a ring.   9 stitch   9 stitch

37 square meshes

Thumb   15 stitch

7.5 cm/20 rows

34. Shown in page 66

You'll need: Crochet cotton gold DMC No. 40, 30g white (298)
Steel crochet hook:
Crochet hook No. I
Making instructions:
First, work motif for back part of glove,
Make clusters of 3-tr and ch-5 ring. Cut thread off. Make 3 more similar pieces of motifs, and join them together. Around 4 joined motifs, work loops of ch on Row 1 and clusters of tr on Row 2. Cut thread off. Then, work ch-151 around the wrist. Make 25.5 loops of ch-5 to make it Row 1. From Row 2, join both sides of 4 motifs with sc and dc as shown. Work plainstitch until Row 34 where motifs are joined. Finish joining motits on Row 34. Work loop st from Row 35. Make ch for thumb at Row 27. Stitch in the 7th loop with sc. Continue to work loops for 4 fingers. Skip loop for a little finger on Row 10, and work 1st row of other 3 fingers. Finish working 3rd finger and begin working a middle and an index finger. Work edging around wrist scooping opposite sts of beginning ch. Work 7 clusters in every 4th loop, and 1 cluster in 4 loops.

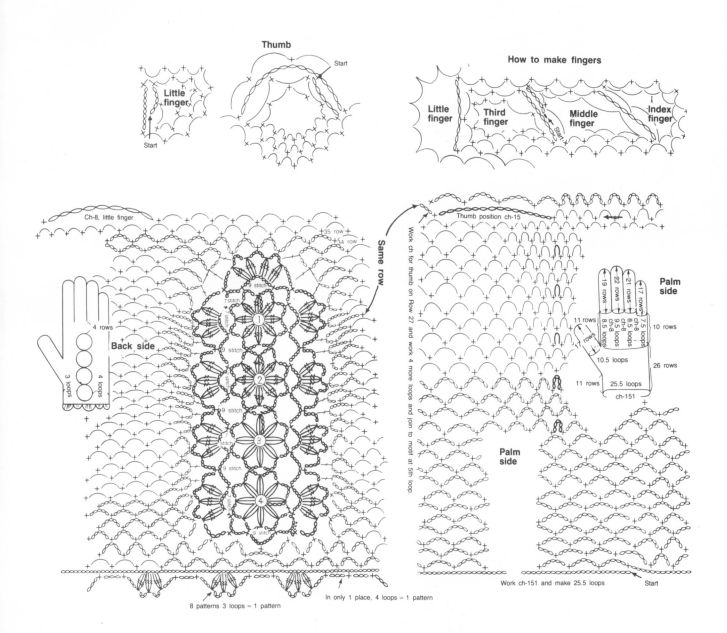

Thumb

How to make fingers

Little finger · Third finger · Middle finger · Index finger

Ch-8, little finger

35 row
34 row

Same row

4 rows

Back side

3 loops · 4 loops

1
2
3
4

9 stitch
7 stitch
9 stitch

8 patterns 3 loops = 1 pattern

In only 1 place, 4 loops = 1 pattern

Work ch for thumb on Row 27 and work 4 more loops and join to motif at 5th loop.

Thumb position ch-15

Palm side

19 rows · 22 rows · 21 rows · 17 rows
ch-8 · 8.5 loops · ch-8 · 9.5 loops · ch-8 · 7.5 loops
11 rows · 10 rows
11 rows
10.5 loops · 26 rows
11 rows · 25.5 loops
ch-151

Palm side

Work ch-151 and make 25.5 loops · Start

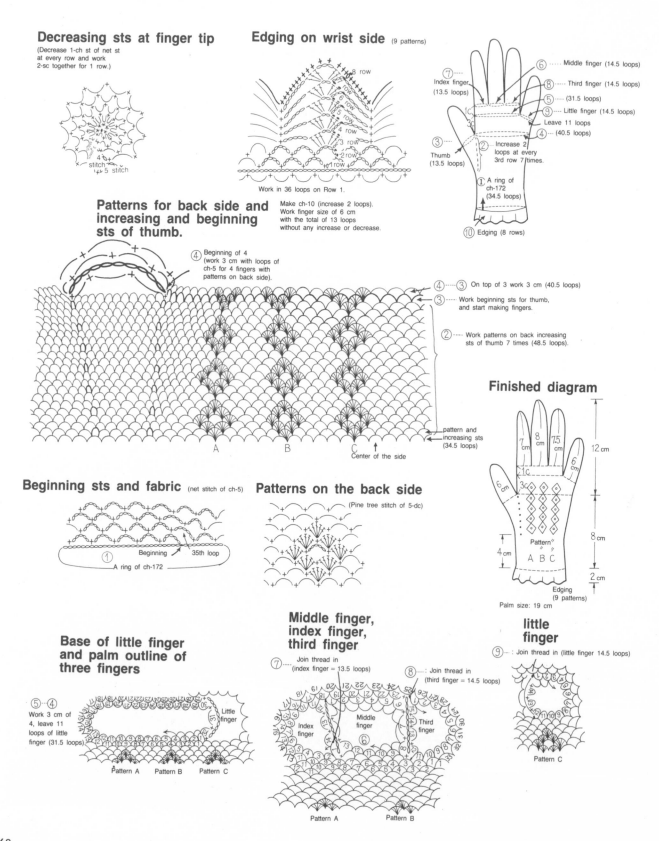

Decreasing sts at finger tip
(Decrease 1-ch st of net st at every row and work 2-sc together for 1 row.)

4 stitch
5 stitch

Edging on wrist side (9 patterns)

8 row
7 row
6 row
5 row
4 row
3 row
2 row
1 row

Work in 36 loops on Row 1.

Make ch-10 (increase 2 loops). Work finger size of 6 cm with the total of 13 loops without any increase or decrease.

⑦ Index finger (13.5 loops)
⑥ Middle finger (14.5 loops)
⑧ Third finger (14.5 loops)
⑤ (31.5 loops)
⑨ Little finger (14.5 loops)
Leave 11 loops
④ (40.5 loops)
③ Thumb (13.5 loops)
② Increase 2 loops at every 3rd row 7 times.
① A ring of ch-172 (34.5 loops)
⑩ Edging (8 rows)

Patterns for back side and increasing and beginning sts of thumb.

④ Beginning of 4 (work 3 cm with loops of ch-5 for 4 fingers with patterns on back side).

④⋯③ On top of 3 work 3 cm (40.5 loops)
③⋯ Work beginning sts for thumb, and start making fingers.
②⋯ Work patterns on back increasing sts of thumb 7 times (48.5 loops).

pattern and increasing sts (34.5 loops)

A   B   C
Center of the side

Finished diagram

7 cm   8 cm   7.5 cm   6 cm   12 cm
1C
3C
Pattern   8 cm
A B C
4 cm
Palm size: 19 cm
Edging (9 patterns)   2 cm

Beginning sts and fabric (net stitch of ch-5)

① Beginning   35th loop
A ring of ch-172

Patterns on the back side
(Pine tree stitch of 5-dc)

Base of little finger and palm outline of three fingers

⑤⋯④ Work 3 cm of 4, leave 11 loops of little finger (31.5 loops)

Little finger

Pattern A   Pattern B   Pattern C

Middle finger, index finger, third finger

⑦ Join thread in (index finger = 13.5 loops)
⑧: Join thread in (third finger = 14.5 loops)

Index finger   Middle finger   Third finger
⑥

Pattern A   Pattern B

little finger

⑨⋯ : Join thread in (little finger 14.5 loops)

Pattern C

You'll need:
Crochet cotton No. 60, 30g black
Steel crochet hook:
Crochet hook No. 0.60m/m
Making instructions:
1: Ch-172, sl st in 1st ch to form a ring. Work 4 cm with loops of ch-5. 2: Increase sts in the part of thumb and work patterns on the back part. 3: Work until sts for thumb start increasing. Ch-10, and skip to the next st increase and stitch with sc and continue to work thumb. 4: Join thread to the end of ch of thumb. Make 3 loops on ch, and continue to work 4 fingers. 5: Ch-10, and skip loops of a little finger and work 3 fingers around. 6: Skip third finger and index finger and work only middle finger. 7: Join thread to a ch, work an index finger. 8: Join thread to a loop and work a third finger. 9: Join thread to a loop and work a little finger. 10: Work the beginning sts in the opposite directions. Work 8 rows of edging with 9 patterns.

---

36.   **Shown on page 70**

You'll need:
Crochet cotton gold DMC No. 40, 20g white (298)
Steel crochet hook:
Crochet hook No. I

Making instructions:
Ch-211. Work 13 pineapple patterns. Increase 1-dc in each second st from both ends on every row. From Row 7, increase sts of shells between pineapple patterns. Work net st with picot between shells. On Row 14, work "ch-3, 2-dc," "2-dc, ch-2, 2-dc" for the next shell. Work sl st on the beginning ch. Work sl st at the end and cut thread off. Work 1 row outside to finish.

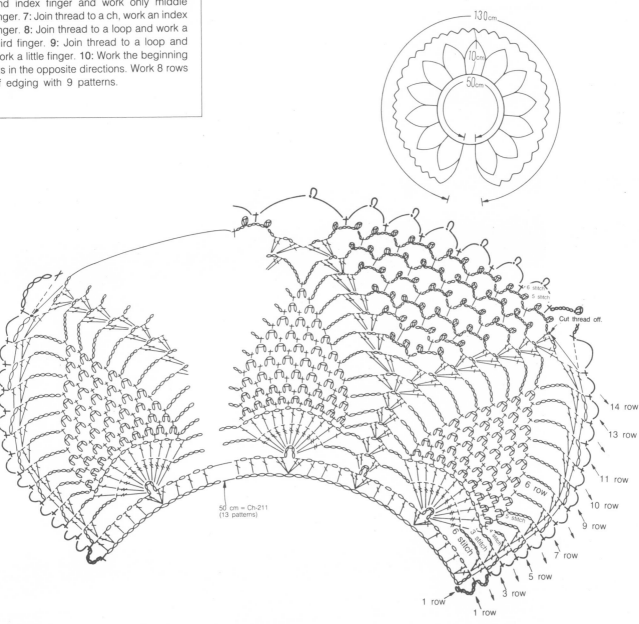

130 cm
10 cm
50 cm

6 stitch
5 stitch
Cut thread off.

14 row
13 row
11 row
10 row
9 row
7 row
5 row
3 row
1 row
1 row

6 row
6 stitch
3 stitch
4 stitch
5 stitch

50 cm = Ch-211
(13 patterns)

FOR ADDITIONAL PLEASURES IN FASHION
Lovely White Collars

Instructions (36) Page 69 (37) Page 72 (38) Page 72

36

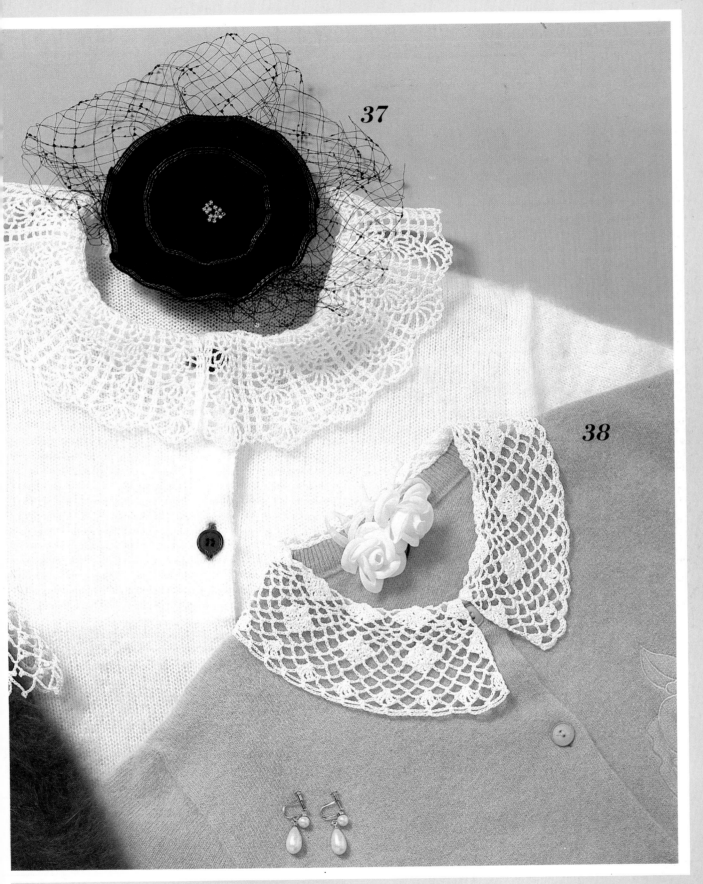

37

38

37. Shown on page 71

You'll need:
Crochet cotton gold DMC No. 40, 15g white (298)
Steel crochet hook:
Crochet hook No. I
Making instructions:
Ch-264. **Row 1:** Ch-3. work a pattern of "2-dc, ch-1, 1-dc, ch-2, 1-dc, ch-1, 2-dc, ch-2." **Row 2:** In accordance with the chart, work "3-dc" at both ends. Work open patterns and net st of "2-dc, ch-2, 2-dc." Repeat above. **Row 9:** Work tr in open pattern instead of dc. **Row 13:** Work dtr in open pattern instead of tr. **Row 14:** Work net st of "1-sc, ch-4." Break off. Work 1 row of sc on beginning ch from the opposite side.

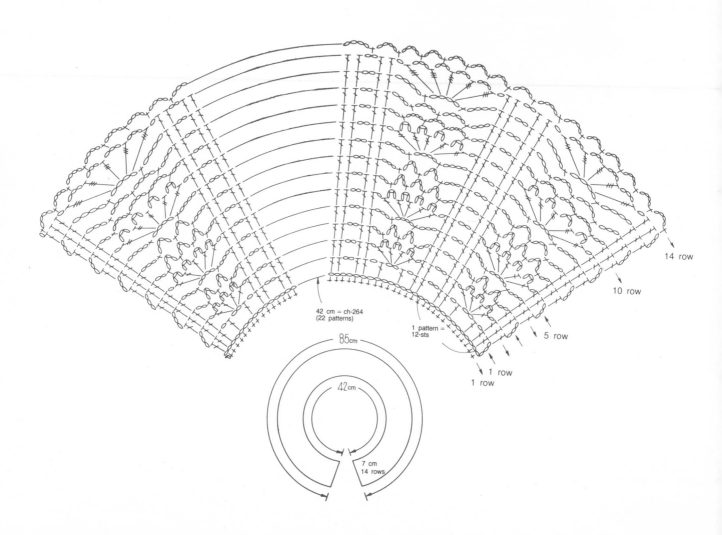

42 cm = ch-264 (22 patterns)

1 pattern = 12-sts

85cm

42cm

7 cm 14 rows

14 row

10 row

5 row

1 row

1 row

38. Shown on page 71

You'll need:
Crochet cotton gold DMC No. 40, 10g white (298)
Steel crochet hook:
Crochet hook No. I
Making instructions:
Ch-154. Work "1-sc, ch-5" to make 36 loops. **Row 2:** Ch-3, work "2-dc" in each sc on the previous row, net st of "sc-1, ch-5" twice, 1-sc, work shell of "2-dc, ch-1, 2-dc" in sc on the previous row. **Row 3:** Repeat 1 net st and 2 shells on both sides of shells on the previous row. **Row 4:** Work the same as on Row 2. **Rows 5 – 7:** Work net st increasing 1 net st at every 4th net st on Row 5 to make 48 net sts. **Row 8:** Work 6-ch sts in net st. **Row 14:** Work "2-tr, 1-ch, 2-tr" instead of shell. **Rows 15, 16:** Work 2 rows of net st. End by working sc on beginning ch from the opposite side.

39.

Shown on page 74

You'll need:
Crochet cotton gold DMC No. 40, 10g
white (298) white beads
Steel crochet hook:
1 Cover toughing shuttle
Crochet hook No. I

Making instructions:

Work with one thread. Begin with central
motif. Work motif in the order of A, B, C, D.
Cut thread off. Make 10 pieces of these.
Insert thread in beads and work A'. Insert 4
beads in 2-p of B as shown. Work C' and D'
joining to next motif. When 10 motifs are
linked, work 3rd round of A" and B". Hold
the collar inversely. Join thread to outside
p and work 4 rows on the neck side of the
collar. In order to make the neck part even,
adjust the length of sts. Break off.

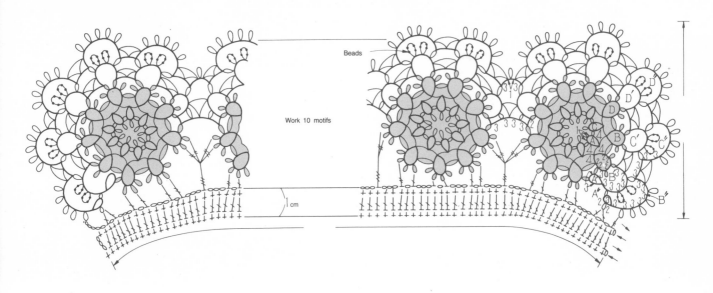

Beads

Work 10 motifs

1 cm

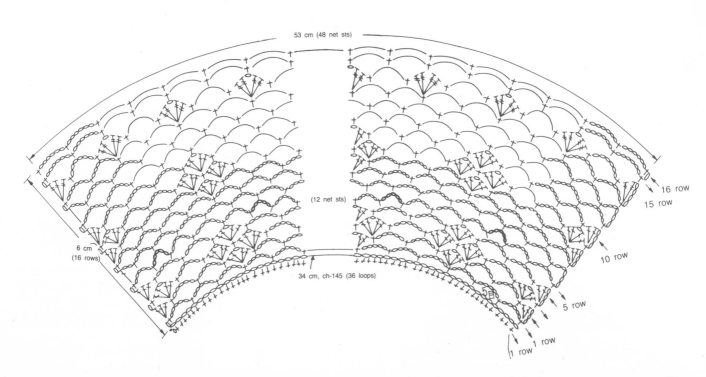

53 cm (48 net sts)

(12 net sts)

6 cm
(16 rows)

34 cm, ch-145 (36 loops)

16 row
15 row

10 row

5 row

1 row 1 row

Lovely White Collars
Instructions (39) Page 73 (40) Page 86

39

40

You'll need:
Crochet cotton gold DMC No. 40, 40g white (298)

Steel crochet hook:
Crochet hook No. I

Finished size: 32 cm in diameter

Making instructions:
Ch-8, sl st in 1st ch to form a ring. **Row 1:** Ch-4, 29-tr in ring, sl st in 4th st of beginning ch. **Row 3:** Make hexagon. **Row 4:** Work the base for pineapple pattern in each corner. Work 12 pineapple patterns with net st between them. **Row 25:** Cut thread off. Join a new thread in and work from Row 26 to Row 30 ending with a loop of ch-3, tr on every row.

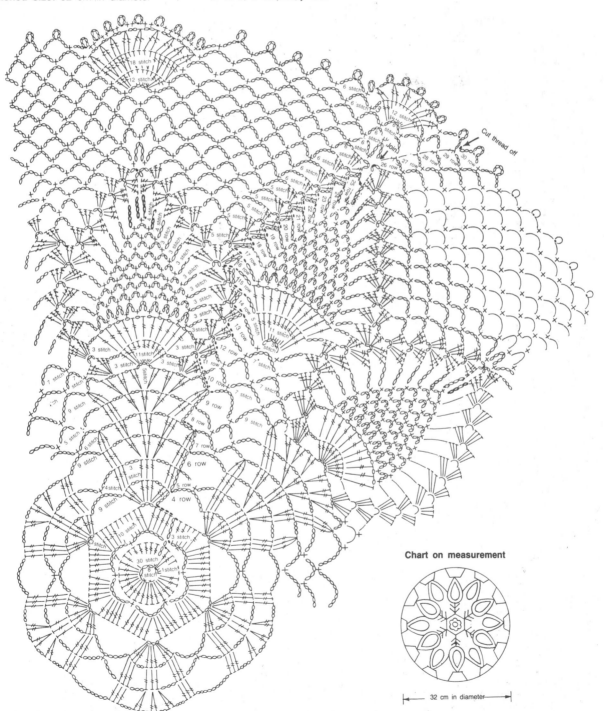

Chart on measurement

32 cm in diameter

2.

Shown on page 4

You'll need:
Crochet cotton gold DMC No. 40, 80g white (298) for 3 pieces

Steel crochet hook:
Crochet hook No. I

Finished size:
Large 43 cm in diameter, medium 33 cm, small 23 cm

Making instructions:
Large — Ch-12, sl st in 1st ch to form a ring. **Row 1:** Ch-4, 27-tr in ring, sl st in 4th st of beginning ch. **Row 2:** Ch-1, work "sc-1, ch-3" in every other tr 14 times, sl st in 1st ch. **Row 3:** Ch-3, cluster of 2-tr, ch-6, repeat "cluster of 3-tr in a loop of ch-3, ch-6." **Rows 4 – 6:** Work loop of ch-7, ch-8 and ch-9. **Row 7:** Ch-3 work 9-dc in each loop of ch-9 on the previous row (126-sts). **Row 8:** Repeat "work 1-sc in dc on the previous row, ch-3," in every 3rd dc around. End with ch-1, 1-hdc. **Row 9:** Ch-3,

"work '1-dc, ch-3, 1-dc on top of next dc, 1-dc in the same loop' in loop of ch-3." Repeat above. **Rows 10 – 19:** Work in the same manner as for Row 9 increasing sts of ch (9-ch sts on Row 19). **Row 20:** Ch-3, 1-dc, ch-2, 2-dc, ch-7, "'2-dc, ch-2, 2-dc' (shell) in a loop of ch-9 on the previous row, ch-7" 41 times. **Row 21:** Work "shell in shell, ch-5, 10-tr in the next shell on the previous row, ch-5, shell in the next shell, ch-7" 14 times. **Row 22:** Repeat "shell in shell, ch-3, '1-tr, ch-1' in tr 9 times and 1-tr, ch-3, shell in shell, ch-5."

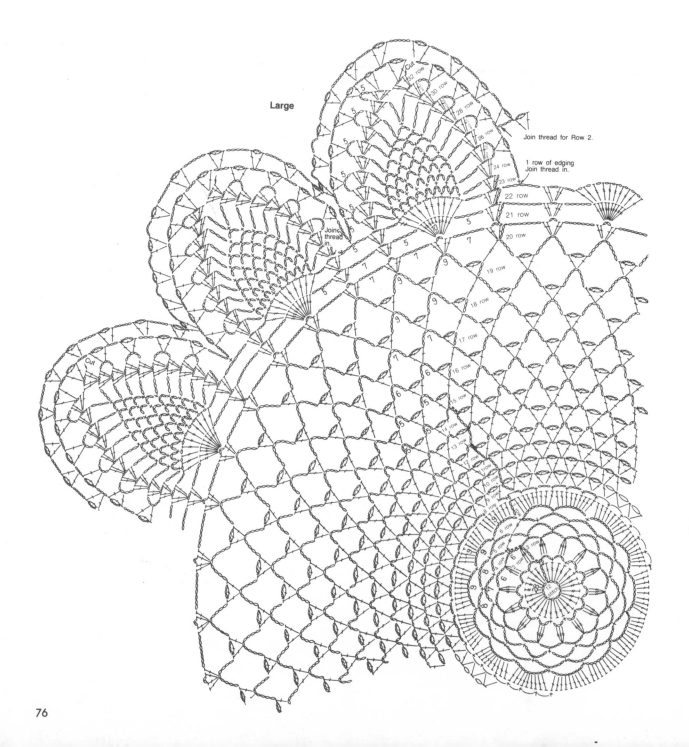

Large

Join thread for Row 2.

1 row of edging
Join thread in.

Row 23: Work each pattern separately. Work shell in shell, ch-3, 8 loops of ch-3 in '1-tr, ch-1' on the previous row, ch-3, shell.

Row 24: Ch-5, turn the cloth, work in the same manner as the previous row decreasing 1 loop of ch-3 at the center. **Rows 25 – 32:** Make a loop of ch-5 for beginning. Shift. Work in the same manner as for Rows 23 and 24 decreasing 1 loop of ch-3 at a time. Work the remaining 13 motifs in the same way.

Edging — Row 1: Join thread to the center of ch-5 on Row 22. Work 1-sc, ch-5, and repeat "'1-dc, ch-3, 1-dc on top of dc, 1-dc in the same loop in a loop of ch-5', ch-3." Work ch-5, 1-sc, ch-5 in between pineapple patterns. Cut thread off. **Row 2:** Referring to the chart, join thread to ch-3 and repeat '1-dc, ch-3, 1-dc on top of dc, 1-dc in the same loop' ch-5 around.

Medium — Work in the same manner as large doily. **Row 1:** Work 30-tr in ring. **Row 16:** Start working pineapple patterns. Work 10 pineapples in the same way as large doily. Work 2 rows of edging.

Small — Work according to the chart. Work pineapple patterns from Row 7. Work 7 pineapples in the same way as a large doily and 2 rows of edging.

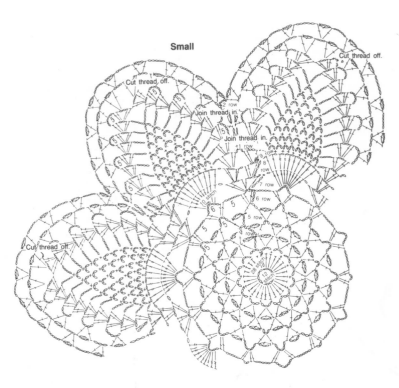

Small

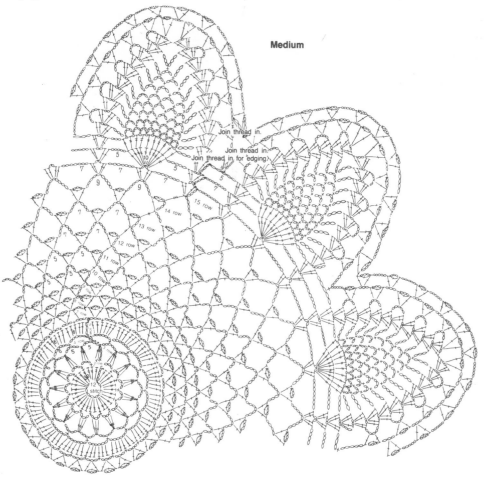

Medium

77

You'll need:

Crochet cotton gold DMC No. 40, 40g white (298)

Steel crochet hook:

Crochet hook No. I

Finished size: 42 cm in diameter

Making instructions:

Make a loop at the end of a cotton. **Row 1:** Ch-3, 15-dc in loop, sl st in 3rd st of beginning ch. **Row 2:** Ch-3, 1-dc, ch-11 (2-dc, ch-11) 7 times. **Row 3:** Ch-3 and 3-dc in a loop of ch-11, ch-3, 4-dc, "4-dc in a loop of ch-11, ch-3, 4-dc" 7 times. **Rows 4 – 8:** Ch-3, work dc in dc and ch-3.

Repeat the same on every row. **Rows 9 – 19:** Work pineapple patterns with clusters of 3-dc between patterns on Row 1 to Row 8, and work filet net st between clusters. **Rows 20 – 32:** Begin to work pineapple patterns with 13-dc in net st (1-sc, ch-9) on Row 19. Work sl st at the end of every row and some more sl sts before beginning the next row.

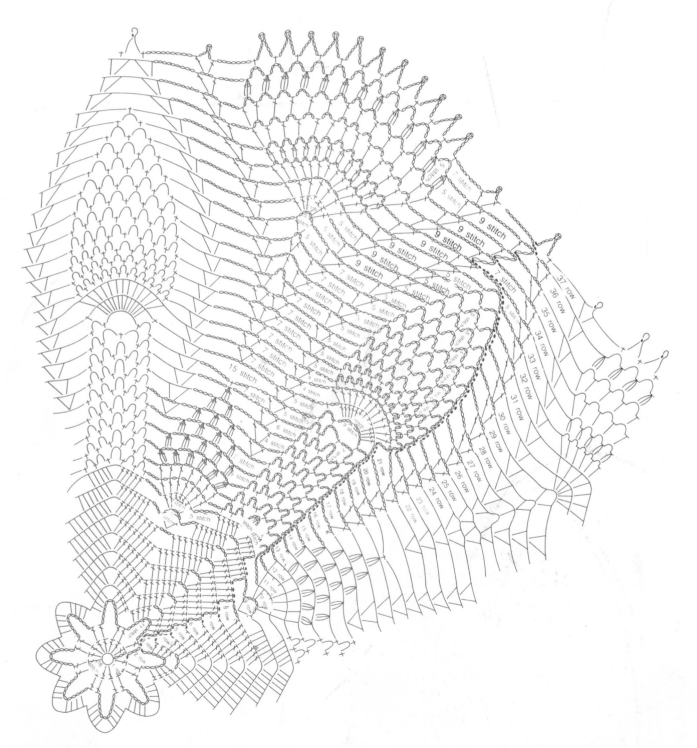

4.

Shown on page 6

You'll need:
Crochet cotton gold DMC No. 40, 30g white (298)
Steel crochet hook:
Crochet hook No. I
Finished size: 32 cm in diameter
Making instructions:
Ch-10, sl st in 1st ch to form a ring. **Row 1:** Ch-6 (1-dc, ch-3) 9 times in ring, sl st in 3rd st of beginning ch. **Row 2:** Ch-3, 3-dc, ch-2 (4-dc, ch-2) 9 times. **Row 3:** Ch-6, work "5-dc, ch-3" in ch-2 on the previous row around. **Row 4:** Ch-1 1-sc, a loop of ch-9 around. **Rows 5, 6:** Work 10-sc and 11-sc in loops (108-sc). **Row 7:** Ch-6, "1-dc on 1-sc, ch-3, skip 2-sc" 35 times. **Rows 8, 9:** Work dc and ch in the same manner as the previous row. **Rows 10, 11:** Make a loop of ch-3 (72 times). **Row 12:** Ch-3, 1-tr, ch-3, ch-5, (1 inverted Y shape st in 2 loops on the previous row, ch-5) 35 times. **Row 13:** "'3-tr, ch-1, 3-tr' in ch-5 on the previous row, ch-6, 1-sc in 3rd inverted Y shape st, ch-6, skip next ch-5." Repeat above. **Rows 14 – 18:** Work tr and ch following the chart. **Row 19:** Work a loop of ch-3 on "1-tr, ch-1" on the previous row 10 times, with ch-5, 6-tr between loops. **Rows 20 – 31:** Work in the same manner as previous row. Decreasing 1 loop of ch-3 at each row, work loop of ch between patterns (12 patterns around). **Rows 32, 33:** Work loop of ch-8 and ch-9 to finish.

6. **Shown on page 8**

You'll need:

Crochet cotton gold DMC No. 40, 120g white (298)

Steel crochet hook:

Crochet hook No. I

Finished size:

81 cm in diameter

Making instruction:

Ch-6, sl st in 1st ch to form a ring. **Row 1:** Ch-5 (1-dc, ch-2) 7 times. **Row 2:** Ch-3, 1-dc, ch-3 (3-dc in 1-dc, ch-3) 7 times. **Row 3:** Ch-11, 1-dc in 3rd ch, ch-7, "1 Y shape pattern st (wind thread around hook 3 times, slip 2 sts each 4 times in the same manner as dc, ch-5, 1-dc in the place of 2nd winding), ch-7" 7 times. **Rows 4 – 10:** Work tr on ch-5 of Y shape pattern st. Work beginning ch for pineapple pattern on Row

10. **Rows 11 – 16:** Make 8 patterns of small pineapple. On top of 7-tr, divide tr into three parts, left, center and right. At the center, work puff st from Row 12. On Row 16, work clusters of 8-tr. **Rows 17 – 21:** Make patterns on clusters of 8-tr. **Rows 22 – 27:** Working net st, make 1 puff each in 8 places on Row 23 and Row 25. **Rows 28 – 43:** Make pineapple patterns on puff st of Row 25, and work "3-tr, ch-5, 3-tr (new pattern)" at the center loop between puffs. On Row 33, work 4-tr between pineapple and new patterns. Start making 16 pineapple patterns with popcorns. **Rows 44 – 52:** Work small pineapple patterns between pineapple patterns with popcorns. **Row 53:** Work 1 row of net st.

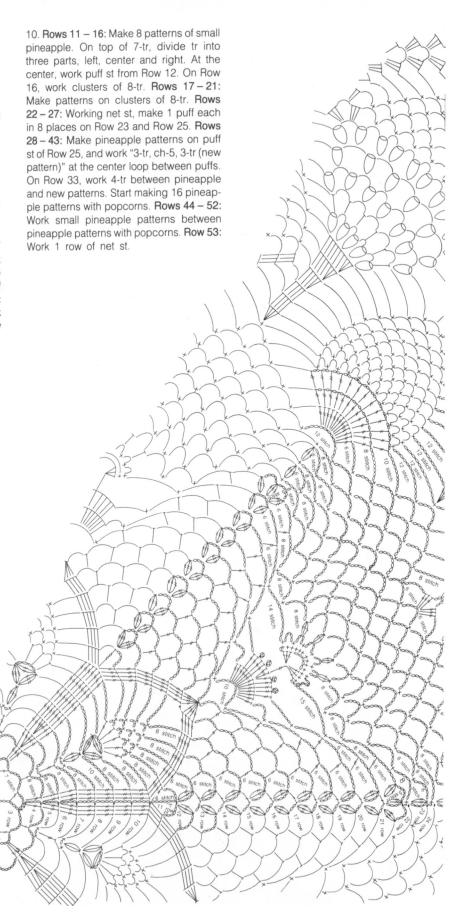

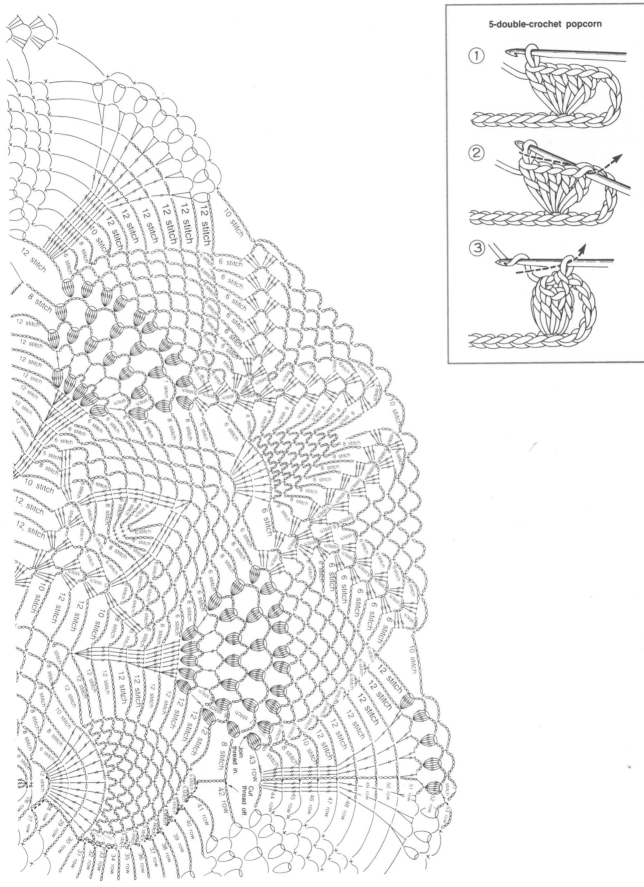

5-double-crochet popcorn

① ② ③

5.

Shown on page 7

You'll need:
Crochet cotton gold DMC No. 40, 20g
white (298)
Steel crochet hook:
Crochet hook No. I
Finished size: 23 cm × 31 cm
Making instructions:
Ch-8, sl st in 1st ch to form a ring. **Row 1:**
Ch-3, 23-dc in ring, sl st in 3rd st of
beginning ch. **Row 2:** Ch-3, 1-dc, 1-dc,
ch-2 (2-dc on dc on the previous row, ch-2

ship 1-dc) 11 times. **Row 3:** Ch-3, 1-dc,
ch-2 2-dc in the same loop, repeat "2-dc,
2-ch, 2-dc" (shell). **Row 4:** Work shell on
shell, ch-2, 12 times. **Row 5:** Work "shell,
ch-4, '2-dc, ch-5, 2-dc' in shell on the
previous row, ch-4" 6 times. **Row 6:** Work
shell, ch-3, 13-tr in ch-5 on the previous
row, ch-3, 6 times. **Row 7:** Work in the
same manner as previous row. Repeat
"1-tr, ch-1." **Row 8:** "Shell, ch-3, 11 loops of
'1-sc, ch-3' in ch-1, 1-sc, ch-3" twice, shell,
ch-2, increasing st by working 2-dc in a
same st (same for the opposite side).
Repeat "shell, ch-3, 11 loops of '1-sc, ch-3'
in ch-1, 1-sc, ch-3." **Rows 9 – 12:** De-

crease 1 loop at every row, while increasing shells at upper left and lower right as
indicated in the chart. **Row 13:** Work each
pattern separately, shell, ch-3, 6 loops of
'1-sc, ch-3,' ch-3, shell. **Rows 14 – 18:**
Ch-4, turn, shell, ch-3, '1-sc, ch-3' (decrease 1 loop on every row), ch-3, shell.
Row 19: Work shell, ch-3, 1-sc, ch-3, shell.
End with ch-4, 1-sc. Cut thread off (1
pineapple is finished). Join thread in for the
next pineapple referring to the chart. Work
in the same manner and cut thread off
where indicated.
Edging — Work 2 rows of edging in
accordance with the chart.

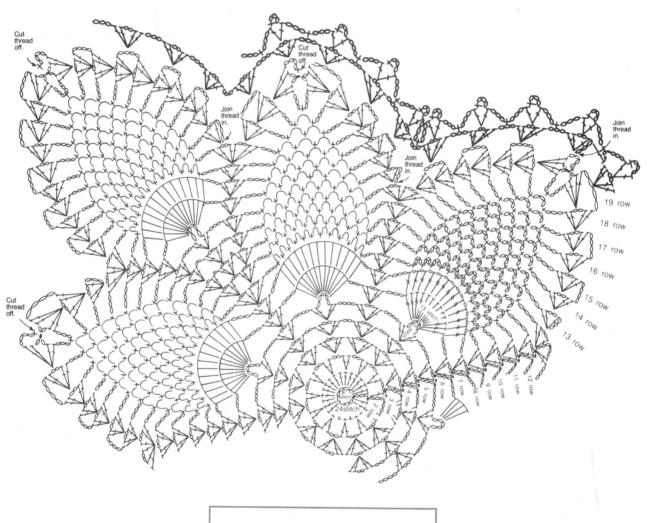

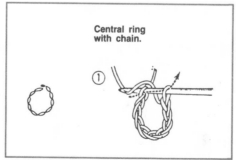

**Central ring
with chain.**

82

You'll need:

Crochet cotton gold DMC No. 40, 160g ivory (206) White embroidery cloth 40 cm by 150 cm

Steel crochet hook:

Crochet hook No. 12

Finished size:

61 cm × 193 cm

Making instructions:

Work in U shape in the order of A, B, C and join them to 3 folded loop (3 fold) with another thread.

(A) Row 1: Ch-14. Work '3-tr, ch-2, 3-tr' in the 5th st. Row 2: Ch-7, 3-tr, ch-2, 3-tr in ch-2. Rows 3 – 257: Repeat the same as Row 2 to work 219 cm in length.

(B) Row 1: Join thread to a loop of Row 1 of A. Work "<3-tr (ch-4 for the beginning), ch-2, 3-tr> once, 'ch-9, 1-sc in the next loop' 3 times, ch-9, << <3-tr, ch-2, 3-tr> once, ch-3>> twice" 4 times on 37 cm side. At corners work '<3-tr, ch-2, 3-tr> once, ch-5, <3-tr, ch-2, 3-tr> once, ch-3' in loop on Row 49 of A. Work <3-tr, ch-2, 3-tr> once in loop on Row 51, ch-3, and repeat "<3-tr, ch-2, 3-tr> once, 'ch-9, 1-sc in the next loop' 3 times, ch-9, << <3-tr, ch-2, 3-tr> once in the next loop, ch-3>>

twice" 13 times to work on 145 cm side (13th repeat will complete on Row 207). Work '<3-tr, ch-2, 3-tr> once, ch-5, <3-tr, ch-2, 3-tr> once, ch-3' of Row 49 in a loop of Row 209 to make a corner. In loops on Rows 211 – 257, repeat Rows 1 – 47 inversely to work last side. Row 2: Ch-5, turn the cloth, and work "3-tr, ch-2, 3-tr, ch-12 in ch-2, 5-dc in 2nd loop, 1-dc in sc, 5-dc in the next loop, ch-12, <'3-tr in ch-2, ch-2, 3-tr' ch-3> twice" 4 times. At corners, work [['3-tr in ch-2, ch-2, 3-tr' once, ch-1, '3-tr, ch-2' in ch-5 twice, 3-tr, ch-1, '3-tr, in ch-2, ch-2, 3-tr' once, ch-3]]. Then, repeat sts marked with " " on other two sides. At corners, work sts indicated in [[ ]]. Rows 3 – 5: Work in the same manner as Row 2. Work sc on Row 3 in dc on Row 2, dc on Row 4, sc on Row 5 decreasing 1st each at both ends of every row. Increase ch-3 on Row 3 between '3-tr in ch-2, ch-2, 3-tr' to be ch-5 on Row 4 and ch-7 on Row 5. On Row 5, work ch-5 instead of ch-2 in sts bracketed in ' '. Row 6: Ch-5, work "'3-tr in ch-2, ch-2, 3-tr' once, ch-12, 3-sc in the center of 5-sc, ch-12, repeat sts indicated in ' ' once, ch-7, 13-dtr in ch-5 on the previous row (beginning sts of pineapple patterns), ch-7" repeatedly. Work 1 pattern of beginning sts for pineapple patterns at corners. Row 7: Work 1-sc in sc-3 on the previous row, and '1-tr, ch-1' in dtr. Row 8: Ch-5, work "'3-tr in ch-2, ch-2, 3-tr, ch-7'

twice, '1-sc in ch-1 on the previous row, ch-5' 11 times, 1-sc in ch-1 at the end, ch-7" repeatedly. Work 1 pattern of sts marked with " " at corners from this row. Rows 9, 10: Work '1-tr, ch-2, 1-tr' in ch-7 one Row 8. Row 11: Work '1-tr, ch-5, 1-tr.' Decrease 1 loop of pineapple pattern at every row. Row 12: Ch-5, repeat "'3-tr in ch-2, ch-2, 3-tr' once, ch-5, '1-tr, ch-2' 7 times and 1-tr in ch-5 on the previous row, ch-5, '1-tr, ch-2' once, ch-8,' 1-sc in a loop of ch-5, ch-5' 7 times, 1-sc in the next loop, ch-8." Row 13: Ch-5, "'3-tr in ch-2, ch-2, 3-tr' once, ch-5, <1-dtr in 1-dtr, sc 4-ch-p, ch-1> 7 times, 1-dtr in dtr, ch-5, sts marked with ' ' once, ch-8, '1-sc in ch-5, ch-5' 6 times, 1-sc in the next ch-5, ch-8" repeat. Rows 14 – 18: In accordance with the chart, increase sts of ch between dtr while decreasing 1 loop from each row. Row 19: Ch-5, work 1 pattern of "'3-tr in ch-2, ch-2, 3-tr' once, ch-10, <1-tr in 1-tr, ch-6, sc 4-ch-p, ch-5> 7 times, 1-tr in 1-tr, ch-10, sts indicated in ' ' once, 1-str in a loop of ch-5". From 2nd pattern, work '3-tr in ch-2 on the previous row, 1-dc in ch-2 of sts marked with " ", 3-dc' and repeat sts bracketed in " ". Row 20: Ch-5. Work '3-tr in ch-2, ch-2, 3-tr' once, ch-12, <1-tr in 1-tr, ch-7, sc 5-ch-p, ch-7> 7 times, 1-tr in 1-tr, ch-12, 3-tr at the foot of dc, ch-2, 3-tr." Repeat. End cloth pattern with sts marked with ' '.

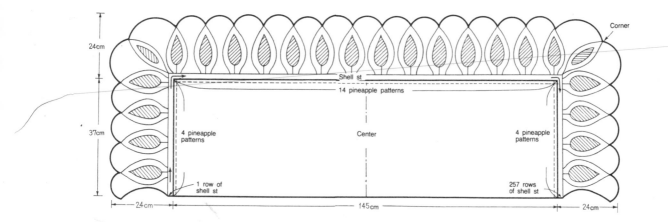

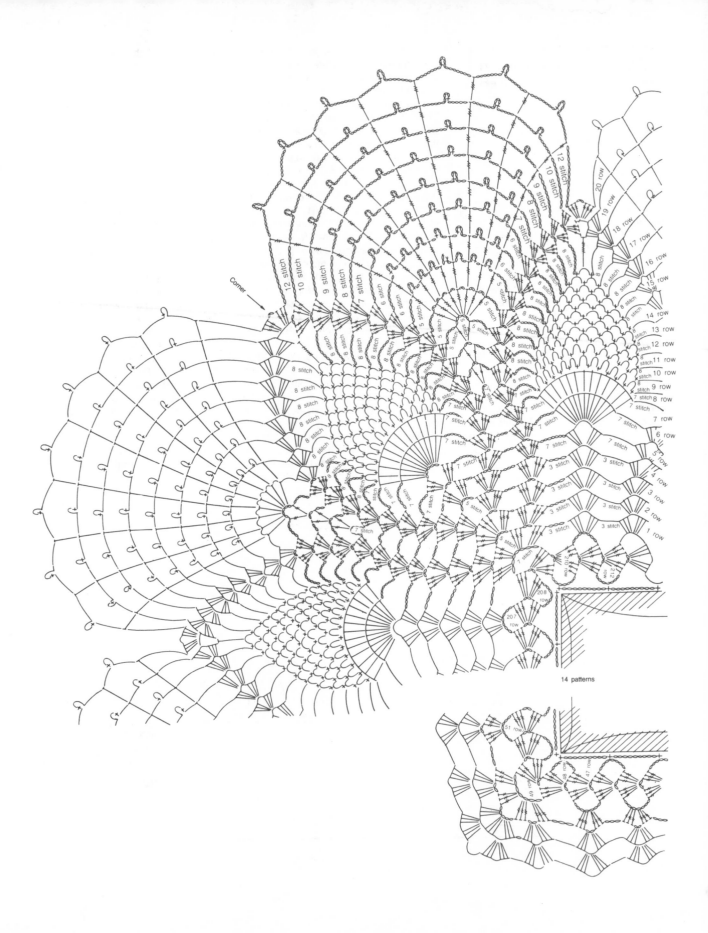

Corner

12 stitch
10 stitch
9 stitch
8 stitch
7 stitch
6 stitch
6 stitch
5 stitch
5 stitch
5 stitch
5 stitch
8 stitch
8 stitch
8 stitch

12 stitch
10 stitch
9 stitch
8 stitch
8 stitch
7 stitch
6 stitch
6 stitch
5 stitch
5 stitch
5 stitch
5 stitch
8 stitch
8 stitch
8 stitch

20 row
19 row
18 row
17 row
16 row
15 row
14 row
13 row
12 row
11 row
10 row
9 row
8 row
7 row
6 row
5 row
4 row
3 row
2 row
1 row

7 stitch
7 stitch
7 stitch
7 stitch
7 stitch
7 stitch
3 stitch
3 stitch
3 stitch
3 stitch
3 stitch
3 stitch
3 stitch

5 stitch

212 row
210 row
208 row
207 row

14 patterns

51 row
49 row
47 row

84

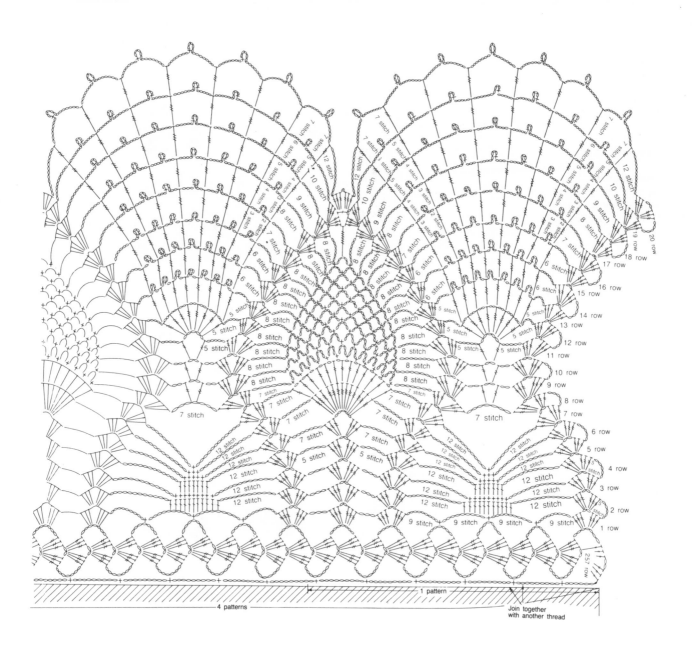
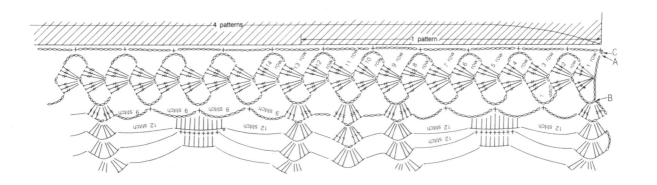

18. Shown on page 35

You'll need:
Crochet cotton gold DMC No. 40, 250g
white (298)
Steel crochet hook:
Crochet hook No. I
Finished size:
56 cm – 143 cm
Making instructions:
Row 1: Ch-304 (56 cm). Ch-5, 1-dc in 9th st
from the hook, repeat "ch-2, 1-dc in 3rd ch"
100 times to make 101 square mesh. **Row
2:** Ch-3, repeat "ch-2, 1-dc in dc on
previous row" 101 times. **Rows 3 – 60:**
Referring to the chart, work "ch-2, 1-dc" for
white square mesh, work 3-dc for square
mesh marked with × to make edging and
inside patterns. **Rows 61 – 195:** Work 3 or
2 horizontal flower patterns alternately.
Rows 196 – 255: Work patterns for Row 1
to Row 60 inversely (56 cm × 143 cm).
Edging — Work 8-sc in each square mesh
at corner, and 3-sc each in other square
mesh.

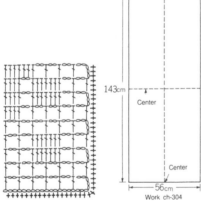

40. Shown on page 74

You'll need:
Daruma crochet cotton gold No. 40, 10g
white (298), 172 iridescent beads, 1 Clover
touching shuttle

Steel crochet hook:
Crochet hook No. I
Making instructions: `
Work 13 motifs with one thread. Work in the
order of alphabet. When M is finished, go
on to N and then on to the next motif. Thus,
work half of motif every time. After finishing
the 13th motif, return to 12th motif. Finish
motif one by one in this way. Insert thread

through beads. Join thread to p. Start
working from A' and join to the top of p.
Insert 4 beads each to picot in places
indicated. Turn the collar. Work edging on
neck side. First, work p, adjusting the
length of dc to make the curve line even.
Then, work sc on 2nd row, dc on 3rd row
and sc on 4th row.

You'll need:
Crochet cotton gold DMC No. 40, 90g ivory (206)

Steel crochet hook:
Crochet hook No. J
Finished size:
37 cm × 54 cm
Making instructions:
Ch-247 (including beginning ch). Start working from Row 4 of design diagram (81 square mesh). Work 113 rows increasing and decreasing sts to make chevron pattern at both ends. Then work 3 rows of chevron patterns at edge decreasing sts. At the edge of beginning ch, join thread to the ch of beginning ch, and work chevron patterns similar to the ones on the edge at 6 places. Work each piece separately.

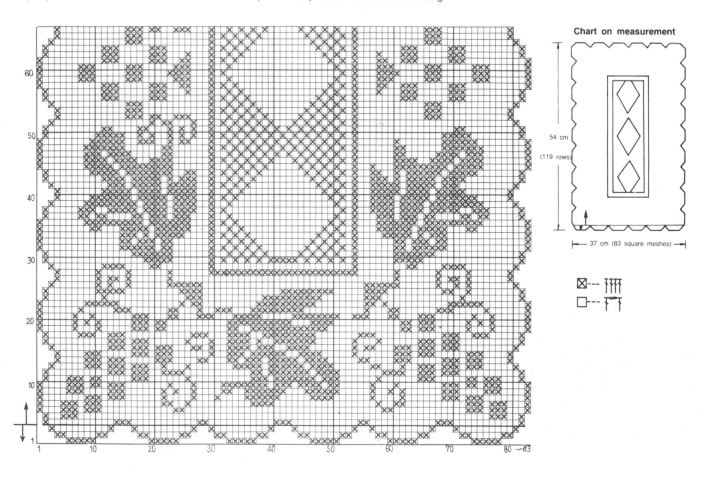

Chart on measurement

54 cm

(119 rows)

37 cm (83 square meshes)

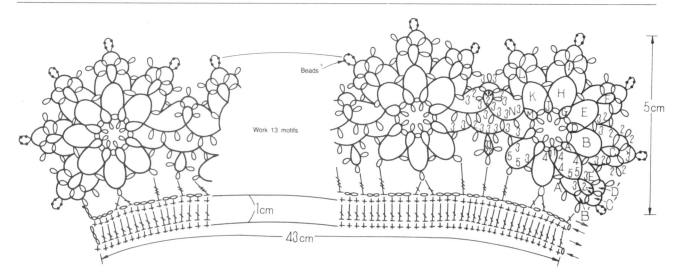

Beads

Work 13 motifs

5cm

1cm

43cm

TO FINISH CROCHET LACES NEATLY

Now, you are finished with the enjoyable and patient work of your crochet. But there is one more step. Finishing perfects your crochet lace. Finishing can make each stitch neater. For those lazy people, here are some simple and easy methods.

Choose the one you think best, based on the condition of your work, its application to your crochet pattern and to your own working style.

A. If A Crochet Lace Finishes Beautifully.

If your crochet is clean and its stitches are neat, iron out immediately because the more the lace is washed, the more it is whitened, but the more it loses its gloss. Use sharp rustless pins and a soft padded surface ironing board to prevent damages to stitches.

(1) Put a board on which guide lines are drawn on the ironing board. Place a transparent vinyl over it.

How to draw guide line:

First, mark the center of a circle, and draw a circle according to the finished size. Divide radius into 3 – 5 parts and draw inner circles depending on the size of the work. Then, draw division lines according to the number of patterns made radially. For example, if there are 6 patterns around, draw 6 division lines. The more there are guide lines, the more the work will be finished neatly. However, sometimes it may become difficult to identify the stress on patterns. Therefore, you have to decide how many lines to draw based on characteristics of the work.

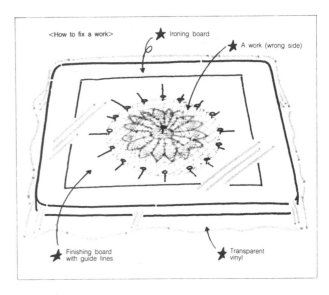

<How to fix a work>   Ironing board   ★ A work (wrong side)

★ Finishing board with guide lines   ★ Transparent vinyl

(3) If you like soft finishing, spray water over the work and adjust the warp of stitches and shapes of picot or net. The order of work in this case is from large to small, such as whole to parts, parts to details and details to stitches. If you like a hard finish, apply starch. A spray type starch is convenient, but before using sprayer, check to see if there is any rust on the spray nozzle, or any other problem in spraying.

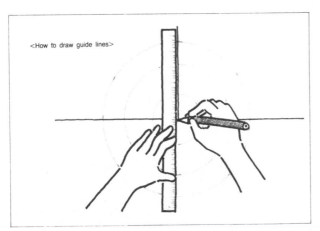

<How to draw guide lines>

(2) Turn over the work and put it on the guide line board. First, pin at the center. In order to make the pattern divide evenly, pin the work in accordance with the guide lines, pulling carefully. Pay attention to design, such as straight or curved lines. When it is evenly stretched, remove the center pin before ironing.

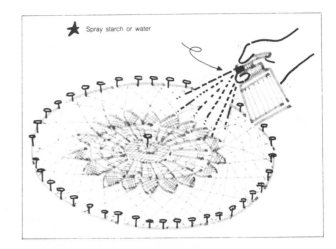

★ Spray starch or water

(4) Apply a cover cloth. Press it from above with iron at high temperature to dry and fix stitches. Be careful not to burn the work. If you move the iron, it may make stitches uneven and pins will have no effect. Remove pins after the work is completely dried.

Finished sizes of doilies and centerpieces indicated here are those sizes measured after they are stretched and fixed in finishing. Therefore, the crocheted size is smaller than the finished size.

(3) Put a finishing board on the ironing board. Place a vinyl over it, and turn over the work on it. Pin it in the same manner as for a neatly worked crochet. Since crochet thread is cotton, it shrinks when it is washed. Stitches and whole crochet will look stiff and shrunken. Therefore, fix the center tightly and pin it, pulling strongly toward outside.

(4) Dry it in airy place. When it is 80% dried put a cover cloth over it and iron by just pressing over the cloth. Be careful not to move iron over the fabric. Remove pins after the piece is completely dried.

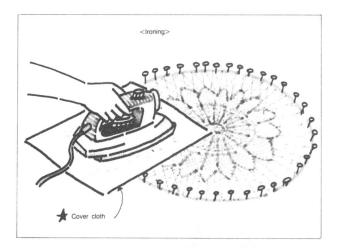

<Ironing>

★ Cover cloth

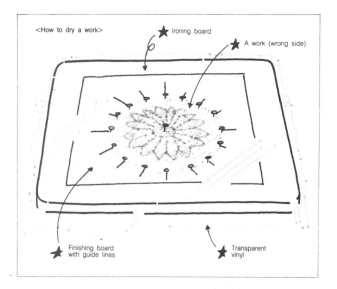

<How to dry a work>

Ironing board

A work (wrong side)

★ Finishing board with guide lines

★ Transparent vinyl

B. If There Are Unwanted Gathers Or If A Crochet Turns Inside Out.

When there are some puckers or if a work turns inside out due to uneven stitches, finish in the same manner as for a neatly worked crochet: Pin it closely. If stitches are short in length compared with its width, it is inclined to cause puckers or gathers. In such a case, try to enlarge the work when completed. If stitches are long in length compared with their width, the work begins to turn inside out. In this case, try to stretch the width of the work.

● Where there are stains and spots on fabric

In removing stains and spots, the quicker the better. Whenever you find stains, remove them as soon as possible.

(1) If it is a small stain, place a work on a towel and tap it with a cloth soaked in soap solution. Stains will be removed easily by changing the position of a towel and tapping repeatedly.

(2) If stains are not prominent, it would come out just by washing. If stains will not be removed easily, soak the work in solution of 1 liter water and 10g neutral detergent. Stains will be removed beautifully when the piece is boiled for 10 minutes to 1 hour, depending on stains.

(3) The rest of the procedure is the same as (2) – (4) of the section, 'If a Work is Dirty.'

C. If A Work Is Dirty

Cleanliness is the essence of crochet lace. Wash the work if it is dirty.

● When it is dirty

(1) Dissolve neutral detergent in tepid water. Wash the crochet lace, shaking or lightly grasping it. Rinse it repeatedly until water becomes clear. Wrap it in a towel and dry.

(2) Since all crochet cotton contains some starch, apply some starch after washing to restore its finish.

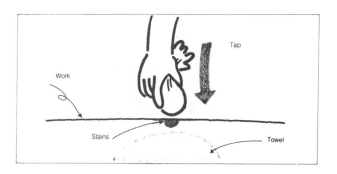

Tap

Work

Stains

Towel

D. How to Make Beautiful Frills

Here is an easy, simple method of making pretty, gorgeous frills.

(1) Fix a work on the ironing board in the same manner as that of 'If a crochet finishes beautifully.' At that time, parts of frills are tightly stretched lengthwise.

(2) Apply thicker starch on frills than on central part. Spray starch in two stages, since it is difficult to dry if it is sprayed all at once.

(3) If it is dried, apply a cover cloth and iron lengthwise on it. Remove pins.

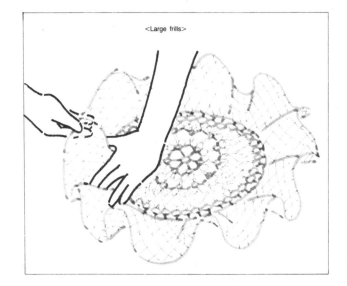

\<Large frills\>

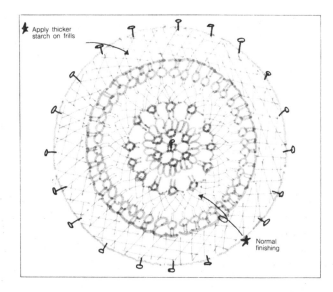

Apply thicker starch on frills

Normal finishing

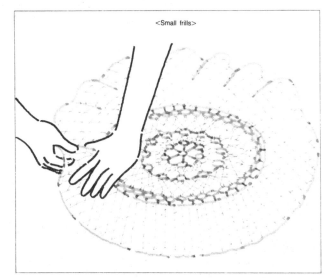

\<Small frills\>

(4) Decide the number and position of frills according to pattern. When frills are large, the number of frills should be small. If frills are small in size, increase the number of them. Turn the fabric right side out. Handle frills with special care. Put the thumb and index finger of the left hand on the inside part of frill positions. Hold and stretch the fabric upward toward outside with the right hand, adjusting the shape with your thumb. When all frills are made, adjust outside fabric with finger tips.

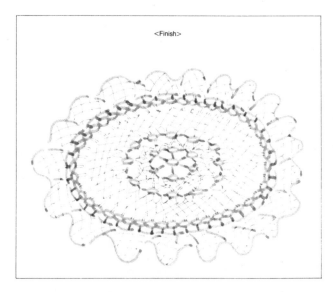

\<Finish\>